EMPATH AND NARCISSIST BOOK

LEARN HOW TO HEAL, DEAL, AND THRIVE.

MICHELLE JULIE FOSTER

WELCOME TO YOUR JOURNEY OF EMPOWERMENT

If you've ever felt submerged in another's feelings or found yourself drained after connecting with someone, know you're not alone. I've deeply felt every interaction, connection, and unspoken sensation, just as you might have. The world's emotions, sometimes overwhelming and intense, often became my own. I remember those times I'd retreat, trying to comprehend why a mere conversation left me so exhausted or why I could sense the undercurrents of feelings others seemed oblivious to.

You see, walking the path of an empath has its highs and lows. And just like you, I've grappled with the allure and challenges of being so finely attuned to those around me. But every stumble, every tear, every moment of doubt led to profound revelations that I am eager to share with you in hopes that my journey can illuminate yours.

This isn't just a guide; it reflects my lived experiences, coupled with insights and strategies that have helped me navigate the intricate dance between my empathic nature and a world filled with diverse energies. From recognizing the early signs of toxic bonds to understanding the motives of those who might unconsciously (or consciously) tap into our vulnerabilities, these pages will equip you with the tools to rise above.

The odyssey of an empath, as I've come to learn, isn't about merely surviving; it's about thriving, harnessing our sensitivities, understanding our strengths, and building resilience. And in those moments when the weight of the world seems too much, remember this: your empathic essence is a gift, one that holds the power to heal, deal with, and uncover love within.

As you embark on this exploration with me, consider this book not a linear path but a compass tailored to your personal journey. Start with the chapters that resonate most deeply with your current experiences. If you've felt the sting of gaslighting or the perplexity of encountering a Dark Empath, delve into those sections to gain clarity. If you're keen on discerning how to identify toxic behavior through real case scenarios, that's a path I've illuminated, too. For those moments when you're seeking to recenter and harness your gifts, turn to the strategies and reflections. Bookmark pages that strike a chord, revisit them and let them remind you of your growth and resilience. This isn't a one-size-fits-all guide but a collection of insights you can tailor to fit your narrative. So, as you flip through these pages, craft your unique roadmap and let your intuition guide the way.

As we venture together, know that the promise of overcoming isn't just a distant dream but a promise, a tangible reality, waiting to be realized.

1

EMBRACE YOUR HIGHLY SENSITIVE NATURE

Dive Deep Into The Roots of Empathy

Empathy is more than just an emotion or a fleeting feeling; it's an intrinsic part of who you are. This ability connects you deeply to others and allows you to understand and often absorb the emotions and energies around you. To fully grasp the complexities of the relationships and situations you encounter, especially those involving narcissists, it's essential to start by understanding your foundational trait – empathy.

Historically, empathy has played a pivotal role in human connection. While living in closely bonded groups, our ancestors relied on this intuitive ability to interpret and anticipate the feelings of their peers. Such insights were vital in fostering community bonds, detecting potential threats, and working cohesively for the collective benefit.

Science traces the roots of empathy back to *mirror neurons* in our brains. These neurons allow you to resonate with emotions and actions you observe in others, experiencing a myriad of feelings that aren't directly your own. This neural wiring underscores the human tendency for connection and shared experiences.

For you, as an empath, these experiences are magnified. You don't merely recognize another's feelings; you deeply internalize them. Though a remarkable gift, this amplified sensitivity can sometimes be overwhelming, particularly when faced with powerful or negative emotions. Your challenge lies in forging deep connections without losing yourself amidst them.

Some believe that heightened empathy arises from personal experiences and upbringing. However, there's compelling evidence suggesting it's innate. By its design, your brain is particularly receptive to emotional and energetic stimuli, leading you to experience the world in an intensely vivid manner.

In the subsequent sections, we'll delve deeper into understanding our unique empathic nature, setting the stage for recognizing where you stand in the spectrum of empathic abilities and how it impacts your interactions, especially with narcissists.

Explore the Spectrum of Your Empathic Abilities

From my own journey, I've realized that while empathy is our shared bond, it doesn't manifest the same in all of us. Just as my personal experiences have painted unique shades of emotions and understanding in my empathic nature, yours will also have distinct hues and nuances. Empathy isn't a one-size-fits-all trait. It's as varied as the colors of a sunset or the melodies in a symphony. Each of us, in our own way, embodies a specific note or shade, bringing depth and diversity to the collective empathic experience. Every unique manifestation comes with its own set of joys and trials.

For some, empathy might manifest as a gentle tug at the heartstrings when witnessing a poignant scene in a movie or hearing a friend's distressing story. For others, this emotional resonance can be so profound that it transcends mere emotional understanding. It might even involve physical sensations or intuitive insights beyond the ordinary.

One of the first distinctions is between cognitive and emotional empathy. It's the difference between recognizing someone's distress and being engulfed by it.

Cognitive empathy, often likened to perspective-taking, is akin to an analytical understanding of someone's feelings. If we were to draw a parallel with literature, cognitive empathy would be understanding the storyline and characters, yet not necessarily being emotionally invested. For instance, if a friend is heartbroken over a breakup, you, through cognitive empathy, would understand why they feel sad. You'd recognize their need for support and might say, "It makes complete sense you're feeling this way."

Emotional empathy, on the other hand, is diving deep into the pages of that book and feeling every emotion, every twist and turn. Using the same example of a friend's breakup, if you're an emotional empath, you might feel their heartbreak almost as if it was your own. Their sadness might make you teary-eyed, and you might genuinely mourn their lost relationship.

Beyond this basic distinction, some identify as **physical empaths,** individuals who can literally experience the world in a tactile, corporeal way. If someone close to you is unwell or fatigued, you might start exhibiting similar symptoms. Picture this: your colleague at work has been suffering from migraines.

While you've never had them, on a day they're particularly struggling, you start to feel a nagging pain in your temple, almost mirroring their discomfort. This uncanny ability to physically resonate with others defines a physical empath. However, the challenge here is differentiating between emotions and physical sensations that are genuinely theirs and those they're absorbing from their surroundings.

Then, there are **intuitive empaths.** For them, the world is laden with unspoken cues, energies, and underlying emotions. It's like having a built-in radar that picks up on the subtlest shifts in the environment. If we consider a regular gathering or party, while most people would see laughter, conversations, and interactions, an intuitive empath might also pick up on underlying tensions, unspoken sadness, or hidden attractions. If you recognize yourself in this, your intuition is likely so finely tuned that you often find yourself knowing something without knowing how you know it. For instance, you might sense a friend is about to share good news or feel uneasy about a decision without a clear, logical reason.

Each type of empathic ability has its challenges. Emotional empaths, for instance, might find it challenging to watch the news or attend distressing events because they absorb the collective grief or pain. Physical empaths might struggle to differentiate between their bodily ailments and those they pick up from others. Intuitive empaths, while blessed with profound insights, might feel overwhelmed by the sheer volume of unspoken information they receive.

It's a journey of self-discovery, and as you delve deeper, you might find that you resonate with one or more of these descriptions. Recognizing and understanding your specific type of empathy is not about labeling but about empowering yourself. With clarity comes the ability to set boundaries, protect yourself, and use your gift in fulfilling ways rather than draining. Understanding these nuances allows for a more harmonious interaction with the world, where the empath doesn't merely absorb but also enriches, elevates, and enlightens their surroundings.

While the broader spectrum of empathy offers a foundational understanding, it's in the intricate nuances and personal resonances that your true empathic nature comes to light.

Identify and Celebrate Your Unique Empath Type

As you've delved into the broader spectrum of empathy, you might have felt a particular resonance or pull toward certain descriptions or scenarios. This isn't by chance. While empathy is a trait many share, its manifestation in you is unique, shaped by both your inner world and the environments you've encountered. Each empathic type illuminates different facets of your empathic nature, resonating with diverse aspects of your life.

The Emotional Empath

It is perhaps the most common type. Such individuals deeply experience the emotions of others around them. It's not just understanding or being attuned to what others feel - it's genuinely feeling those emotions as if they were their own. If you often find that you're riding the emotional waves of those around you, you might identify as an emotional empath. It's not just about understanding another's feelings but immersing in them, feeling their joys, anxieties, or sorrows as intensely as they do. While this allows for profound connections, it also requires a keen sense of self-awareness to ensure you're not constantly overwhelmed. Consider walking into a room after an argument has taken place. Even if no words are shared about the dispute, an emotional empath might feel a heavy weight or a sudden shift in their mood. They absorb emotional energy from their surroundings, both the joyous and the sad.

Imagine watching a film where the protagonist goes through a heart-wrenching loss. An emotional empath wouldn't just understand the grief; they'd perhaps cry or feel a heavy sorrow themselves, echoing the character's emotions.

The Geomantic Empath

Do certain places call out to you? Whether it's a serene beach, an old building, or even bustling city streets, geomantic empaths (also known as *environmental empaths*) strongly connect with places. They have a fine-tuned connection to the physical spaces and environments around them. They can feel the "vibes" or energies of sites, whether it's a room, a house, or even an outdoor setting.

Visiting historical sites or landmarks can be a particularly profound experience for geomantic empaths. Stepping onto a battlefield from centuries past, they might feel an inexplicable heaviness or sadness. Conversely, they might feel an over-whelming sense of peace and contentment in a serene forest or by a calm lake.

The Animal Empath

If you've always felt a kinship with creatures, understanding their moods, needs, or even fears, you're resonating with this empathic type. Animal empaths have a powerful bond with animals and can often intuit their feelings and needs. This doesn't just apply to pets; it spans across the animal kingdom.

They can sense distress, happiness, fear, and other emotions in animals. With their unspoken languages, animals communicate volumes to those who can truly listen.

Suppose a neighborhood cat is injured or hungry. In that case, an animal empath might be the first to notice, even if the animal doesn't display overt signs. They could walk into a room and instantly connect with a pet, sensing its comfort or discomfort. They're also the kind of individuals who find deep solace in the company of animals, often describing them as their *soul companions*.

The Claircognizant Empath

Intuition takes a front seat for this type of empath. They often possess a clear "knowing" ability. It's not based on feelings or logical deduction; it's a spontaneous insight into events, situations, or even people.

Imagine having a friend who's been dating someone new and is smitten. Upon meeting the new partner, a claircognizant empath might have a sudden, clear insight - "This relationship won't last" or "This person has a secret." There's no evidence, no gut feeling, just a clear knowing. While it can be challenging to navigate these insights, especially when they're unexpected, they often prove to be uncannily accurate.

Recognizing which type of empath you resonate with, or even identifying with multiple types, can provide clarity and understanding about how you interact with the world. These categorizations aren't meant to limit but to empower, allowing you to harness your gifts in the most fulfilling way possible. As you walk your path through your empathic nature, acknowledging these facets will pave the way for deeper connections, not just with others but also with your own self.

In my journey to self-awareness, I've discovered that introspection isn't just a practice—it's an embrace. As I delved into the layers of my empathic nature, I began to see reflections of different empath types within me. Recognizing these shades was not just enlightening; it felt like coming home. It's a profound feeling akin to listening to a long-forgotten melody or finding a piece of yourself you never knew was missing. Every facet, every unique type of empathy, shapes our view of the world, refining our interactions and enriching our experiences. But as with all profound insights, this self-awareness also brings responsibility. Knowing your empath type isn't just about celebration; it's about understanding the balance required to navigate the world.

But as you navigate the complexities of your empathic nature, it's crucial to be aware of potential challenges, especially when these heightened sensitivities intersect with certain personalities and situations. The dance between an empath and a narcissist, for instance, is one such dynamic that requires keen awareness and understanding. Knowing your strengths and vulnerabilities as an empath is the first step in equipping yourself to handle such challenging relationships. It's about cherishing your perceptions' beauty while building resilience against potential overwhelm.

Navigate the Challenges of High Sensitivity

The depth with which you experience the world, while a profound gift, also brings its set of challenges. Like a finely tuned instrument, your heightened sensitivity captures the myriad notes of the world. Still, it can also resonate too strongly, sometimes to the point of overwhelm. Our gift, in essence, is a double-edged sword.

Tuning into the emotions and energies around you often places you at the heart of every situation's emotional landscape. This profound connection can lead to **emotional saturation**. Imagine being a sponge: while it can absorb water up to its capacity, there's a limit. Similarly, in emotionally charged settings, you might reach a point where the overwhelming mix of feelings becomes intense. While the joys can be uplifting, the weight of sorrows and anxieties can be overwhelming, especially when these feelings aren't even your own.

Consider a day in the life of an empath: a colleague shares her struggles with a failing marriage over lunch, a friend texts about feeling depressed, they witness a heated argument between strangers on the street and then come home to a roommate anxious about job security. By the end of the day, the empath might feel drained, overwhelmed, or even display emotions linked to these experiences, feeling a mix of sadness, anxiety, and tension, even if their day was relatively calm.

Furthermore, discerning between your emotions and those of others can become a blurred line. This **emotional entanglement** can be incredibly challenging when faced with strong personalities or those in distress. This fusion of emotions can lead to confusion, exhaustion, and sometimes even a loss of personal identity. It can leave you questioning, "Is this sorrow mine, or am I feeling the remnants of someone else's pain?"

Imagine an empath in a relationship with someone who struggles with mood swings. They feel on top of the world on their partner's good days. On bad days, they plunge into depths of despair. Over time, the empath may struggle to discern their own emotional state independent of their partner. They might even neglect their personal well-being, focusing entirely on the emotional state of their significant other.

Physical environments can also play a significant role. Empaths don't just resonate with people; they can also be receptive to a place's energies. Crowded places, loud noises, or areas with intense emotional histories can become terrifying.

An empath might visit a bustling market. While many revel in the chaos, colors, sounds, and scents, the empath might feel quickly overwhelmed. The mix of emotions from the crowd, the sensory overload from the surroundings can make them feel dizzy, anxious, or eager to leave. On the other hand, places like serene parks or quiet libraries might be where they feel most at peace. Historical places, too, can be a double-edged sword. A centuries-old cathedral might bring feelings of awe and serenity, but a war memorial might immerse them in profound sorrow and grief. Understanding your reactions, especially if you identify as a geomantic empath, is crucial in navigating these spaces.

Our world thrives on a complex tapestry of visible and hidden energies. While many remain oblivious to these forces, you, as an empath, are acutely attuned to them. This heightened sensitivity makes you receptive to overt emotions and the **unseen energies** that permeate spaces, interactions, and objects. Think of them as silent waves radiating from individuals, places, or even past events. Their nature can vary: uplifting, draining, or neutral, yet for empaths, their presence is unmistakable and often profoundly impactful. Be it the aura of a cherished heirloom or the remnants of tension from an earlier disagreement, these energies shape your perceptions and feelings, emphasizing the depth of the world beyond its apparent facade.

Consider an empath attending an estate sale. While others might see only the physical items and their monetary value, the empath might pick up on the energies imbued within these objects. A vintage wedding dress might emanate a profound sense of joy and nostalgia, while an old portrait might exude sadness or longing. Similarly, walking into an old building might make them feel like they're stepping back in time, experiencing snippets of emotions, stories, and energies from people long gone.

Another instance might involve being in nature. While everyone can appreciate the beauty of a forest, empaths might feel the vibrant life force energy of the trees, plants, and animals around them. It's like tuning into a frequency where every living thing communicates its essence, story, and vitality.

These unseen energies can be both a gift and a challenge. They enhance the depth we perceive the world, enabling profound connections with history, nature, and life's essence. However, constant exposure can be draining, especially to negative or intense energies. Recognizing the influence of these energies is pivotal for us as empaths. It explains certain unexpected feelings or sensations and provides strategies for self-protection. With this insight, we can thoughtfully engage with uplifting environments and be wary of those that may deplete our energy. This discernment becomes an invaluable tool in navigating the intricacies of daily life.

As we come to understand and embrace the depths and nuances of our empathic nature, it becomes clear that this beautiful gift also requires vigilance. The same sensitivity that allows us to resonate with others' emotions and experiences can also make us susceptible to certain individuals who might not have our best interests at heart. While navigating the challenges of high sensitivity is essential, it's equally vital to be aware of those who might exploit our empathic abilities. This leads us to the realm of narcissists, individuals who, with their unique charm and manipulative tendencies, can present challenges for empaths. Let's delve deeper into understanding these personalities and learn how to unmask them, ensuring our emotional safety.

2

UNMASK THE NARCISSIST AROUND YOU

Unearth the Origins and Traits of Narcissists

In your path to understanding and navigating the world of heightened sensitivity, you must grasp the nature of narcissists who stand in sharp contrast to empaths. I've often encountered the enigma of the narcissist. At their heart lies a unique interplay of self-importance, a hunger for admiration, and often a surprising fragility masked by outward confidence.

Historically, the term *narcissism* draws its roots from the Greek myth of Narcissus, a young man who, upon seeing his reflection in a pool, becomes so enamored that he cannot tear himself away, leading to his tragic demise. While this tale paints a picture of self-obsession, understanding modern-day narcissism requires a deeper exploration.

At the core of a narcissist's psyche is an **inflated sense of self-worth,** often appearing excessively confident and self-assured. They perceive themselves as exceptional, even if they lack the accomplishments to back such beliefs. This isn't mere confidence; it's a deep-seated belief in their superiority. While self-confidence is typically seen as a positive trait, in narcissists, this often crosses over into arrogance and superiority. They believe they are special and often seek validation and admiration from others to confirm this belief.

Consider, for instance, James, a colleague at work. Every team meeting, he turns the conversation towards his achievements, even if they're irrelevant. He can't tolerate anyone outshining him and often belittles others to keep himself on a pedestal.

Yet, this exterior often hides an **internal vulnerability.** Deep down, many narcissists harbor insecurities and fears of inadequacy. Their grandiose behavior often acts as a defense mechanism, a protective facade to shield them from these internal vulnerabilities. They're extremely sensitive to criticism, no matter how constructive, and can become defensive or even aggressive when confronted. This vulnerability is rarely, if ever, shown to the world. Instead, it's masked by their outward display of superiority. This dichotomy is pivotal in understanding their interactions and motivations.

Take Sarah, a friend who always appears confident and often boasts about her life's perfection on social media. However, when she received minor feedback on a project, she overreacted, lashing out and isolating herself for days, showcasing her hidden vulnerabilities.

Interpersonal relationships become complex arenas for narcissists. They tend to seek relationships that bolster their ego, where they are perpetually in the limelight. They often lack genuine empathy, struggling to understand or connect with the emotions of others. Instead, relationships often become transactional, primarily focusing on what they can gain: admiration, validation, or other benefits.

Furthermore, a narcissist's sense of **entitlement** is unparalleled. They genuinely believe they deserve special treatment and will often become impatient or angry if they don't receive it. Boundaries are often overlooked, with a propensity to overstep or disregard the needs and feelings of others. This can manifest in various ways, from expecting preferential treatment in social settings to believing they are above the rules that apply to everyone else.

For example, consider Mike, a neighbor who always parks his car in a no-parking zone. When confronted, he simply remarked, "Those rules aren't for people like me." This blatant sense of entitlement makes it challenging for others to address or correct his behavior.

It's also essential to differentiate between traits of narcissism and *Narcissistic Personality Disorder (NPD)*. While many might display narcissistic characteristics to varying degrees, NPD is a diagnosable mental health condition characterized by pronounced narcissistic behaviors causing significant impairment in interpersonal relationships and daily functioning.

Take Emma, who often showcases narcissistic traits, like craving admiration and struggling to empathize with others. However, she doesn't fit the clinical criteria for NPD as these traits don't severely disrupt her life or relationships. On the other hand, with diagnosed NPD, Robert has lost multiple jobs and relationships due to his persistent narcissistic behaviors, indicating a more severe and ingrained pattern.

Understanding these nuances is crucial. Labeling someone a *narcissist* without acknowledging the depth and range of this behavior can oversimplify and misrepresent the issue. Recognizing these traits and understanding their origins is the first step in navigating interactions with narcissists. This knowledge acts as a shield, allowing you to engage with awareness, spotting behaviors and patterns that can otherwise go unnoticed. But recognition is only the beginning. The true challenge lies in guarding yourself against the allure and manipulations often accompanying such personalities. As you move forward, equipping yourself with the tools to safeguard your emotions and maintain your ground becomes paramount.

Guard Against the Narcissist's Charm and Manipulations

The allure of the narcissist can be both powerful and perplexing. Masked beneath their veneer of confidence and charisma lies a web of tactics designed to draw you in and, often, maintain an upper hand in the relationship.

The Initial Charm

Narcissists are often masters of first impressions. Their self-assured nature and talent for conversation can make them incredibly captivating. They might compliment you, flatter your qualities, and paint a genuine picture of understanding. This phase, often termed *love bombing*, involves showering the person with excessive affection, attention, gifts, and compliments to win them over and gain their trust rapidly. This sudden overflow of love can feel intoxicating and overwhelming, making the recipient feel incredibly special and unique. However, this isn't genuine affection; it's a strategy used to control and manipulate.

The reason love bombing is so effective is because of its intensity. The constant messages, the unexpected gifts, and the seemingly undivided attention can make anyone feel like they're on cloud nine. It creates a powerful emotional bond that can be hard to break free from, even when other more manipulative or abusive behaviors start to emerge later on. In essence, love bombing acts as a smokescreen, hiding the narcissist's true intentions and making it difficult for the person on the receiving end to see the relationship clearly.

Example: Sophie met Jake at a mutual friend's party. They instantly connected, and Jake didn't waste any time. Within a week of their meeting, he had already sent her flowers and organized surprise dates. He bombarded her with affectionate messages throughout the day. He constantly shared how he felt they were "soulmates" and "destined to be together." This was like a whirlwind romance straight out of a movie for Sophie. She felt cherished and thought she had finally found someone who genuinely appreciated her.

However, as weeks turned into months, Jake's behavior began to change. Once he felt secure that Sophie was committed to the relationship, the endless compliments dwindled, replaced by subtle criticisms. If Sophie ever brought up concerns, Jake would reminisce about their early days and how they were "meant to be." This reference to their initial intense phase kept Sophie second-guessing her feelings and judgments, making her more susceptible to further manipulative tactics.

Mirroring Your Desires

One of the narcissist's most potent tools is their ability to reflect what you want to see. They are adept at reading people and identifying their desires, dreams, and insecurities. Mirroring these back creates an illusion of a deep connection, making you feel seen, understood, and valued. When someone reflects our actions and beliefs, it can generate feelings of trust and rapport. We're naturally drawn to individuals like us, so it's easy to mistake this for genuine connection when someone echoes our sentiments or mimics our behaviors. However, with narcissists, this act isn't rooted in authenticity. It's a deliberate and calculated strategy to lure someone into their web. While it's natural for partners or friends to pick up on each other's habits over time, narcissists' intentional mimicking is devoid of genuine attachment or affection. Recognizing this tactic is crucial to avoid being trapped by a narcissist's façade of compatibility.

Example: Let's take the case of Liam and Maya. Maya, an enthusiastic art lover, often visited art galleries on weekends. When she met Liam, on their first date, she spoke passionately about her love for Renaissance art. Liam, quick to catch on, mentioned how he had always been fascinated by the Renaissance period too, even detailing a faux visit to Florence where he was "enthralled" by the masterpieces. He mirrored her enthusiasm, favorite artists, and thoughts on various art pieces.

Maya, impressed by their shared passion, felt an immediate connection. They began spending more time together, with Liam always echoing Maya's opinions, whether about movies, food, or political views. It seemed they were perfectly in sync. However, as months passed, Maya began noticing inconsistencies in Liam's stories. She discovered he had never been to Florence, and his previously expressed political solid views would shift based on the people he was talking to.

For Maya, the realization came when she noticed Liam

mirroring another friend's behaviors right before her, adopting interests and views he had never mentioned before. The impeccable alignment of their likes and dislikes wasn't a fortunate match; it was a mirage crafted by Liam to draw her in.

Subtle Undermining

As the relationship progresses, the initial charm gives way to subtle digs and underminings. What was once overt admiration might transform into passive-aggressive comments, backhanded compliments, or even blatant criticism. This shift is jarring, especially when juxtaposed against their initial adoration, leaving you second-guessing your perceptions and values. Unlike overt and aggressive put-downs, subtle undermining is insidious, often going unnoticed until significant emotional damage has been done. This tactic aims to shake an individual's confidence and self-worth, making them more pliable and dependent on the narcissist for validation. It is especially dangerous because it masquerades as genuine concern or innocent commentary. It requires a discerning eye and strong self-awareness to detect and counteract.

It can take various forms, from backhanded compliments to feigned concern or thinly veiled sarcasm. It's designed to plant seeds of doubt, making the recipient question their abilities, feelings, and even sanity. Over time, these subtle digs can erode one's self-esteem, making them more susceptible to further manipulation and control.

Example: Consider Elena, a talented pianist who recently landed a spot in a prestigious music academy. Her narcissist partner, Mark, felt threatened by her achievement, fearing he would lose control over her. Instead of overtly discouraging her, he took a more subtle route.

After one of Elena's performances, Mark approached her with a smile, saying, "You did great, considering how little time you had to prepare." While the compliment appeared genuine on the surface, the latter part of the sentence subtly implied that her performance was lacking. Another time, when Elena practiced a challenging piece, Mark casually remarked, "Are you sure that's the right tempo? It sounds slightly off to me, but what do I know?" Again, a feigned concern masked as innocent feedback.

Though seemingly insignificant, such words began gathering in Elena's mind. She started doubting her skills, second-guessing her choices, and becoming overly critical of her performances. Unbeknownst to her, Mark's subtle undermining had its intended effect: Elena began seeking his approval and validation, her self-worth intricately tied to his feedback.

Control and Dependence

Narcissists thrive on control. They'll often seek to establish a dynamic where you depend on them emotionally, financially, or socially. They might isolate you from friends or family, monopolize your time, or even belittle your achievements, all in an attempt to create a narrative where they are indispensable. The essence of such control is the narcissist's need to diminish the autonomy of others, ensuring they remain the dominant figure.

Example: Let's take the case of Allison and Alex. They've been in a relationship for two years. Alex, displaying traits of narcissism, has a significant influence over many aspects of Allison's life. He often decides where they go, who they meet, and even what she should wear. He swiftly finds ways to bring her back under his control if she ever attempts to exert her independence.

For instance, Allison once expressed a desire to join a book club, hoping to reconnect with her love for literature and make new friends. Alex's immediate response was dismissive, questioning the 'kind of people' who attend such clubs and insinuating they might negatively influence her. Instead, he suggested they start watching a new TV series together during that time.

Over the weeks, whenever the book club topic arose, Alex would emphasize how much he valued their 'exclusive' TV time, making Allison feel guilty for even considering another engagement. If she persisted, he'd switch tactics, reminiscing about past moments where Allison 'abandoned' him for other interests, painting himself as the victim.

Feeling trapped between her desires and not wanting to hurt Alex, Allison eventually gave up on the book club idea. This outcome was precisely what Alex wanted: maintaining his control over her time, her activities, and, ultimately, her life.

The Cycle of Push and Pull

One of the trademarks of a narcissistic relationship is the unpredictability. There are moments of intense affection followed by cold withdrawals, keeping you in a constant state of flux. This push-pull cycle is both disorienting and binding. The moments of warmth and affection become lifelines, making the cold phases even more challenging to endure. This roller coaster can lead to feelings of intense love, followed by deep pain and bewilderment, often leaving the victim questioning their worth and reality.

Example: Consider Lisa and Robert. In the beginning, Robert showered Lisa with attention and admiration. He made her feel special like she was the only person in the world who mattered to him. This was the "pull." Lisa felt cherished and loved, creating a deep bond.

However, once Lisa felt secure and expected mutual respect and understanding, Robert would initiate the "push." He'd become distant, cold, even critical. He'd cancel plans without explanation or become incommunicado for days. When Lisa would confront him, he'd accuse her of being needy or over-reacting.

Just when Lisa would feel the relationship was on the brink, Robert would revert to his earlier loving self, reigniting her hope and passion. This unpredictable pattern kept Lisa in constant emotional flux, yearning for the moments of "pull" while dreading the inevitable "push."

Over time, Lisa began to doubt her own perceptions. Maybe she was too needy? Maybe she had misunderstood Robert's actions? This self-doubt, perpetuated by the ongoing cycle, further entrenched her in the relationship, making it difficult for her to see Robert's behavior for the manipulative tactic it was.

Guarding against these tactics requires a blend of awareness, self-assuredness, and boundaries. Recognizing these patterns as they emerge is the first step. The initial charm, while intoxicating, should be taken with a pinch of salt. Slow down, reflect, and ensure you're not getting swept away in the whirlwind.

Maintaining a strong sense of self is pivotal. While seeking validation in relationships is natural, sourcing your self-worth internally is crucial. The more rooted you are in your value, the harder it becomes for a narcissist to shake it.

Establishing clear boundaries, both emotionally and practically, can act as safeguards. Whether it's the time you spend with them, the personal information you share, or the emotional investments you make, boundaries ensure you're not over-extending or losing yourself in the relationship.

While understanding the narcissist's tactics equips you for the journey, the true depth of the relationship lies in the intricate dance between their nature and your empathic sensitivities. Each step, each twirl, taught me something new, and this dance, with its challenges and epiphanies, became an essential chapter in my journey of self-discovery. This dynamic becomes the next phase of our exploration.

Understand the Dance Between You and the Narcissist

The union of an empath and a narcissist can often resemble a paradoxical dance—a waltz of two opposing forces. On one side, you have the empath's innate desire to understand, heal, and connect, and on the other, the narcissist's quest for validation, control, and admiration. This dance, while compelling, is fraught with challenges and revelations.

At its core, the attraction between the two often stems from a subconscious understanding of what the other offers. As empaths, with our boundless compassion and desire to heal, we are drawn to the hidden vulnerabilities of the narcissist. We sense the pain masked by the bravado, the insecurities shielded by the arrogance. In the narcissist, the empath sees a wounded soul, a project, someone they can help and heal.

Conversely, narcissists are drawn to the empath's endless reservoir of understanding and validation. In the empath, they find a willing audience for their tales, an ever-present source of admiration, and, more importantly, someone who can soothe their internal tumult. The empath's validation feeds the narcissist's need for external affirmation.

Yet, as the relationship deepens, the initial attraction can give way to a series of challenges. Our desire to heal can often lead us to overlook or even justify the narcissist's manipulative tactics. We might find ourselves constantly giving, trying to fill the void we perceive in the narcissist, often at the expense of our well-being.

The narcissists, on their part, might begin to see the empath not as an equal partner but as a means to an end. The empath's compassion becomes a resource they can tap into, manipulate, and exploit. The dynamic can shift from mutual respect to one of control and dependence.

One of the hallmarks of this relationship is the *emotional rollercoaster* it often becomes. The highs are euphoric, with moments of profound connection and understanding. But the lows are equally intense, marked by misunderstandings, manipulations, and emotional withdrawals.

One of the most significant challenges we must face as empaths is *maintaining our sense of self*. In our quest to understand and heal the narcissist, we might find our boundaries blurred and our emotions entangled. The once-clear distinction between our feelings and those of the narcissist becomes muddied.

However, it's essential to understand that while the dynamic is challenging, it also offers growth opportunities. In my personal experiences with such relationships, they often acted as mirrors, reflecting parts of myself I might have overlooked or undervalued. Each interaction became a lesson. These bonds taught me about my limits, reminded me of my worth, and, most importantly, helped me understand and reaffirm my intrinsic value.

As you navigate this intricate waltz, *awareness* remains your most potent tool: recognizing the patterns, understanding the pulls and tugs, and, most importantly, staying rooted in your sense of self becomes crucial. It's also essential to understand that not all narcissists make their intentions or characteristics so blatantly known. Some operate in the shadows, with subtlety, making them even more challenging to identify. This brings us to a particularly elusive type: the covert narcissist. Let's venture deeper into understanding this variant and the unique challenges it presents.

Unmasking the Subtleties of the Covert Narcissist

While many are familiar with the overt narcissist, a counterpart operates with far more discretion and, often, deception. This variant moves silently, almost like a shadow in our lives, making their manipulations harder to pinpoint. As an empath striving for understanding and healing, it's crucial to unmask this hidden face of narcissism. Let's delve into the world of the covert narcissist and uncover the subtleties that define them. Their presentation is an enigma, modest on the surface yet deeply driven by a need for validation.

A Veiled Performance

Covert narcissists aren't the ones basking in the limelight, flaunting their achievements, or openly demanding admiration. Instead, they subtly hint at their perceived inadequacies, waiting for you to console, reassure, or validate them. It's a delicate performance, seeking attention without explicitly asking for it.

The Undercurrents of Manipulation

Interacting with a covert narcissist, especially for someone with heightened emotional sensitivity, can be akin to navigating a foggy maze. They don't wield control with overt force but employ passive-aggressive tactics. These range from sly remarks intended to make you doubt yourself to playing the victim, hoping you'll rush in with empathy and comfort. Their manipulations are so refined they can leave even the most self-aware individuals questioning their perceptions.

The Weight of Hidden Envy

Scratch the surface of their humility, and you'll find a reservoir of envy. They might never express it, but covert narcissists harbor a smoldering jealousy towards anyone they perceive as having what they lack. This envy, left unchecked, can manifest in attempts to undermine or belittle others, especially when they believe no one is watching.

The Victim's Veil

Among their most deceptive tools is their ability to play the victim. They recount tales of challenges, always painting themselves as the misunderstood hero or the perennial victim. For an empath, this tactic is particularly ensnaring. Your natural inclination is to heal, help, and comfort. Yet, with covert narcissists, this very strength can become a vulnerability if they exploit your compassion.

Silent Superiority

Deep within, akin to their overt counterparts, covert narcissists harbor a profound sense of superiority. They believe they're exceptional and deserving of special treatment. But they're also crafty. Understanding that blatant arrogance can repel, they cloak their superiority in humility, revealing it only in guarded moments.

Having unraveled the layers of the covert narcissist, it's clear that understanding the complexities of narcissistic behavior is only half the battle. Being equipped to recognize these behaviors in real time is the shield that protects from further harm. As empaths, our innate sensitivity can sometimes cloud immediate judgment, making it essential to have clear markers to identify potential threats. Whether dealing with overt narcissists, their covert counterparts, or any variant in between, there are universal signs that scream *danger*. And as you deepen this understanding, the next step is to recognize the warning signs early on to safeguard oneself from potential harm.

Spot the 10 Red Flags Before It's Too Late

In the whirlwind of emotions that often accompanies a relationship with a narcissist, it can be easy to overlook the subtle signs that all isn't as it seems. By learning to spot these early red flags, you can protect yourself from deeper entanglement, ensuring that you recognize potential manipulative patterns before they escalate.

1. Overwhelming Flattery. While compliments are a part of any healthy relationship, the narcissist's flattery often borders on excessive. It feels intoxicating, almost too good to be true. Love bombing can be an early sign aimed at pulling you into their sphere.

2. Quick Escalation. Narcissists might push for intimacy or commitment at an alarming speed. Whether it's professing love, sharing deeply personal stories, or envisioning a shared future, this rapid progression can be a tactic to make you feel special and cement their place in your life.

3. Dominance in Conversations. Pay attention to the balance in your interactions. Does the conversation always revolve around them? Are your feelings, thoughts, or concerns often sidelined or dismissed? A continuous focus on their narrative at your expense is a significant red flag.

4. Jealousy and Possessiveness. While a certain degree of jealousy can be a natural part of relationships, with narcissists, it can take on a more controlling tone. They might be overly possessive, not just of your time but also of your other relationships, viewing them as threats.

5. Gaslighting. Even in the early stages, a narcissist might resort to gaslighting—discrediting your feelings, memories, or experiences. Statements like "You're too sensitive" or "That never happened" are indicators that they're trying to shake your trust in your perceptions. We will delve deep into this subject in an entire chapter dedicated to recognizing and countering gaslighting, ensuring you're fully equipped to handle such tactics.

6. Entitlement. Be wary of any signs that they believe they're above others or deserve special treatment. Whether it's cutting lines, disregarding rules, or expecting undue favors, this sense of entitlement can manifest in varied ways.

7. Lack of Empathy. While they might feign concern, narcissists often struggle with genuine empathy. Watch out for moments when they seem indifferent to your distress or belittle your emotions, prioritizing their feelings over yours.

8. History of Turbulent Relationships. If they often speak of past relationships with disdain, portraying themselves as perpetual victims, it's a sign to tread carefully. While everyone has challenging relationships, a continuous pattern might indicate they're the common denominator.

9. Manipulative Behaviors. Even in casual interactions, they might employ tactics to get their way—guilt-tripping, playing the victim, or even subtle threats. Recognize these manipulations for what they are: attempts to control the narrative.

10. Conditional Affection. Their affection often comes with strings attached. If their warmth and care seem conditional, based on your actions or reactions, it's a sign that their love isn't genuine but a tool for manipulation.

By recognizing these early signs, you arm yourself with the knowledge to navigate the relationship cautiously. The key is to *trust your instincts*. If something feels off, chances are, it is. As you equip yourself with this awareness, you're better prepared to delve deeper into understanding the motivations and mechanisms driving these behaviors.

Decode the Narcissist's Motivations

To navigate the intricate web of a narcissist's behavior, we must attempt to understand the driving forces behind their actions. In my interactions, even when their actions appeared erratic or baseless, I realized that there often was a method beneath the apparent madness.

Desire for Control

The desire for control often acts as a cornerstone in the architecture of a narcissist's personality. It is a motivation rooted in the need to dictate terms, sculpt scenarios, and be the puppeteer of situations and people in their vicinity—this longing to control springs from various sources, ranging from personal insecurities to past experiences of powerlessness.

At the heart of this controlling nature is the narcissist's urge to create an environment where variables are predictable, outcomes are as per their design, and the chances of unforeseen challenges or ego bruises are minimized. They instinctively believe that by manipulating situations and individuals, they can prevent potential emotional harm. Digging deeper, some of this behavior can be traced back to traumatic experiences from their past. There may have been moments when they felt intensely powerless, and now, as a defense mechanism, they yearn to dominate their current surroundings to avoid any semblance of that prior helplessness.

Moreover, when a narcissist exerts control, it isn't merely about steering circumstances. It's an act of affirming their self-perceived superiority. Every time they make others bend to their will, it fortifies their elevated sense of self. Their aversion to unpredictability compounds this. The unpredictable is a threat to the narcissist, a challenge to their constructed self-image. Therefore, they meticulously tailor their environment to align with their desires, ensuring they never face any situation undermining their carefully curated self-perception.

Need for Admiration

The narcissist's need for admiration runs deep and serves as one of the cornerstones of their motivation in many interpersonal relationships. This need stems from a profound inner emptiness or a lack of self-worth, even if they never openly admit to or even recognize this void. They constantly seek external validation to fill this internal gap.

Admiration from others acts as a mirror, reflecting a grandiose image of themselves that they desperately want to believe in. Every compliment, every nod of appreciation, fuels their constructed self-image, allowing them to maintain a facade of confidence and superiority. In a way, this external validation is their lifeline, stabilizing their often-fragile self-esteem.

However, this relentless pursuit of admiration has its pitfalls. It makes the narcissist incredibly sensitive to criticism, no matter how slight. Negative feedback, instead of being taken as constructive, is seen as a direct attack on their self-worth. This is why they might react with extreme defensiveness or even aggression when faced with criticism.

Moreover, their dependence on admiration can lead to a transactional relationship approach. Individuals are valued based on the amount of affirmation they provide. Those who cease to admire or, worse, begin to criticize are often discarded or devalued, while those who continually feed the narcissist's need for praise are favored and held in high regard.

In essence, the narcissist's need for admiration is a double-edged sword. While it propels them to achieve often and present themselves in ways that demand recognition, it also makes them vulnerable, tying their sense of self-worth to the unpredictable winds of external validation.

Fear of Inferiority

At the core of many narcissistic behaviors lies a deep-rooted fear of inferiority. This fear isn't always immediately apparent, especially given the narcissist's outward display of confidence and superiority. Yet, it serves as one of the primary drivers for many of their actions and attitudes.

Imagine for a moment the self-perceived world of the narcissist. They are the protagonist in their narrative—unmatched in skill, intellect, and charisma. They've meticulously constructed this self-image and fiercely guard it. However, beneath this grandiose facade is a fragile self-esteem that is hyper-vulnerable to any perception of weakness or flaw. This fear often stems from past experiences—perhaps childhood instances where they felt overshadowed, criticized without compassion, or were held to unattainably high standards. Over time, these experiences mold their perception, leading them to equate their worth with constant superiority.

In relationships and professional settings, this motivation manifests in various ways. This unease drives them to consistently hunt for validation, often fishing for compliments or artfully steering conversations to shine a light on their own achievements. When presented with feedback, their instinctive response might be aggressive or dismissive, especially if it challenges their self-perceived grandeur. They tend to dominate dialogues, ensuring they remain the focal point, always in the spotlight. Moreover, to maintain their self-proclaimed pedestal, they might belittle or undermine those around them, particularly if they view someone as a potential challenge to their sense of superiority.

Understanding the profound impact of this fear allows for a more empathetic view of the narcissist. It's essential, however, to strike a balance between understanding their motivations and ensuring one doesn't become a casualty of their defensive mechanisms.

Desire for Attention

Narcissists deeply desire attention, rooted in their need to be consistently affirmed and acknowledged. This yearning is more than just a mere liking for the limelight; it's an essential component of their self-worth. To a narcissist, attention is not just flattering; it is life-sustaining.

At the core of this motivation is the narcissist's fragile ego. While they may project an image of invincibility or supreme confidence, internally, many narcissists grapple with self-doubt and insecurity. Being the center of attention reassures them of their value and importance in the eyes of others. It's a way of constantly reinforcing their self-belief and warding off those creeping feelings of inadequacy.

This thirst for attention often manifests in their interactions and choices. A narcissist might consistently steer conversations back to themselves, regardless of the topic at hand. They might share glorious tales of their exploits, constantly amplifying their role or importance. They could be prone to posting frequent updates on social media, always seeking validation through likes, comments, and shares. In group settings, they might employ tactics like interruption, one-upmanship, or even theatrical displays of emotion to redirect the focus back to them.

However, their craving for attention isn't just about positive reinforcement. Even negative attention, like conflict or drama, can be preferable to being ignored. For a narcissist, being overlooked or sidelined is the ultimate slight, as it threatens their very self-concept. The desire for attention, thus, isn't merely about vanity or arrogance. It's a complex motivation rooted in a blend of insecurity, self-preservation, and the perpetual need for external validation.

Avoidance of Responsibility

Despite their often-grandiose self-perception, narcissists tend to avoid responsibility, particularly when things go wrong or are less than perfect. This avoidance is not merely a reflection of laziness or indifference. Still, it is deeply rooted in their need to maintain an untainted self-image.

For a narcissist, acknowledging mistakes or accepting responsibility can be tantamount to admitting flaws. This deeply threatens their often-fragile self-concept, which hinges on their superiority and perfection. Admitting errors can shatter this facade, they've so carefully built. Therefore, instead of confronting and owning up to their mistakes, they might deflect blame, point fingers, or create a series of excuses.

Their deep-seated fear of judgment further reinforces this behavior. While narcissists might seem overtly confident or even arrogant, they harbor an intense fear of being perceived as inadequate or inferior. In their view, accepting responsibility for mistakes or failures might offer others a glimpse into their vulnerabilities. This is something they'll go to great lengths to avoid.

In interpersonal relationships, this avoidance of responsibility can manifest in various ways. Narcissists might blame their partner for relational issues, refusing to acknowledge their role in the discord. In a professional setting, they might scapegoat colleagues or subordinates when a project goes awry, even if their own decisions were the primary cause of the failure.

Interestingly, this avoidance is selective. When things go well, the narcissist is more than eager to take credit, often exaggerating their role or contributions. It's only in the face of shortcomings or failures that their aversion to responsibility becomes evident.

This tendency protects their self-image and reinforces their sense of entitlement. By consistently sidestepping responsibility, the narcissist sends a clear message: they are above reproach, regardless of their actions or decisions. This can be incredibly challenging for those around them, as it creates an environment where accountability is one-sided, and the narcissist remains perpetually beyond reach.

The Pursuit of Power

Narcissists often have an insatiable drive for power, deeply interwoven with their self-identity, self-worth, and how they perceive the world around them. For many narcissists, power becomes the yardstick of measuring their worth. They believe that each achievement in their pursuit of power validates their inherent superiority over others.

Yet, beneath this external facade of confidence, many narcissists hide deep-seated feelings of inadequacy. Their aggressive drive for power frequently overcompensates this inner turmoil. By holding positions of influence or exerting control over others, they can, even momentarily, quieten their internal criticism. In doing so, they also ensure a continuous flow of admiration and validation from those around them. Whether in a corporate setting, within a community, or in personal relationships, being powerful means others are bound to look up to them, feeding their ongoing need for validation.

Another fascinating angle to their desire for power is the protection it offers against vulnerability. By being the one in control, they can dictate terms, set the narrative, and, most importantly, avoid situations where they might feel exposed or criticized. Moreover, many narcissists inherently view interactions as hierarchical. For them, life becomes a game where they must always establish their dominance. Achieving power places, them atop this perceived hierarchy, ensuring they always have the upper hand.

Fear of Intimacy

For many, the concept of a narcissist fearing intimacy might seem counterintuitive. Aren't they the ones often pursuing relationships with intense vigor? Yet, delve deeper, and you'll find that their relationship dynamics are a complex tapestry woven with a profound underlying fear of true emotional intimacy.

At the heart of a narcissist's fear of intimacy is vulnerability. True intimacy requires one to bare their soul, expose their flaws, and entrust another with their deepest secrets. For narcissists, this is tantamount to relinquishing control, something they are deeply averse to. They fear that by showing their authentic self, they might face rejection, criticism, or, worse, be deemed *ordinary* or *average*. This terrifies them because it directly conflicts with their inflated self-image and the facade they've built.

While they may dive headfirst into relationships, showering their partners with attention and affection, this display often remains superficial. It's a part of their charm offensive, ensuring they remain in control and are constantly admired. However, when the relationship reaches a point where genuine emotional depth and vulnerability are required, they often retreat, erect barriers, or shift dynamics to avoid exposing their true selves.

Consider a scenario where a partner confides a personal trauma or insecurity to a narcissist, expecting mutual vulnerability in return. Instead of reciprocating with their own genuine feelings, the narcissist might deflect, minimize their partner's feelings, or switch the topic entirely to avoid delving deep into their own emotional landscape.

Their avoidance of true intimacy isn't just limited to romantic relationships. They maintain a calculated distance even in friendships or familial ties, ensuring they never fully expose their emotional core. This protective mechanism shields them from potential hurt or judgment but, in doing so, often leaves them isolated in their emotional cocoon.

Recognizing this fear in narcissists is vital. It offers a lens through which their behaviors can be understood and navigated. However, it's essential to approach this realization with caution, understanding that their internal battles don't excuse the external harm they might cause in their quest to shield themselves from true intimacy.

Understanding these motivations isn't about justifying or excusing their behavior but equipping yourself with the insight to navigate interactions with a narcissist. With this knowledge, you can better predict their reactions, safeguard against their manipulations, and make informed choices about your engagement level.

In my experience with narcissists, I've been on the receiving end of a particularly insidious tactic: gaslighting. This subtle art of manipulation, seemingly harmless at first, began to chip away at my trust in my own perceptions and memories. The more I experienced it, the more I realized the importance of recognizing its signs and countering its effects to shield myself and regain my ground. It's essential to delve deep into understanding its nuances and mechanisms, preparing yourself for recognition and resistance.

3

STAND STRONG AGAINST GASLIGHTING

Define and Recognize Gaslighting's Subtle Tactics

There's a haunting sensation when you begin to question your own reality—a sensation I'm all too familiar with. Gaslighting is a term that, unfortunately, became a part of my vocabulary during a particularly tumultuous relationship. For those unfamiliar, gaslighting is a form of psychological manipulation where the manipulator plants seeds of doubt in the mind of a person or a group, making them question their perception, memory, or even their sanity. The name derives from the play-turned-movie *Gas Light*, where a husband manipulates his wife into believing she's losing her mind.

At first, the signs can be almost imperceptible. Little comments here and there, questioning your recollection of events: "Are you sure that's what happened?" or "You tend to be forgetful; maybe you just didn't remember it right." Though seemingly benign, these comments are the start of a more significant, insidious game.

In my own experience, it began as off-hand comments about how I remembered things, slowly evolving into more direct contradictions of events that I was certain of. For instance, during an argument, they might say, "I never said that," despite me recalling it. Over time, these subtle tactics made me question specific events and my ability to recall and trust in general.

But why do people resort to gaslighting? The answer often lies in a *mix of control and deflection*. In an attempt to maintain control over a situation or relationship, the manipulator uses gaslighting to make the other person doubt themselves, thereby diverting attention away from the manipulator's own behavior. It's a defense mechanism, one that shifts blame and responsibility.

This manipulation can be especially detrimental for empaths or anyone deeply in tune with emotions. We rely heavily on our intuition, feelings, and perceptions to navigate our relationships. When someone deliberately tries to erode that inner compass, it can be destabilizing.

Equipping yourself against gaslighting starts with understanding and recognizing its tactics. A crucial step is building awareness about how they manifest. It could be trivializing your feelings, denying past actions, shifting blame, or projecting their own behavior onto you. Knowledge is power. And in this case, knowledge can be the shield that guards your mind and self-worth.

Trivializing Feelings

One of the most common tactics involves the narcissist belittling or invalidating the emotions and feelings of their victim. When someone says, "Why are you overreacting? It's not a big deal," they are trying to diminish the significance of the victim's experience. This tactic makes the victim doubt the validity of their own emotions, thus ensuring the narcissist remains in control of the narrative.

Denial

Denial is a direct refusal to accept reality. By saying things like "I never said that" or "You must have heard wrong," the narcissist is actively rejecting factual evidence. This confuses the victim and often makes them question their own memory and sanity, allowing the narcissist to manipulate situations in their favor easily.

Shifting Blame

Instead of taking responsibility for their actions, a narcissist will often divert the blame onto the victim. Phrases like "You always want to argue!" or "This wouldn't have happened if you hadn't..." shift the focus and responsibility away from the narcissist's behavior and onto the victim, making them feel guilty for the narcissist's actions.

Withholding Information

Withholding essential details or pretending to be unaware is another tactic to control the narrative. When a narcissist says, "I don't know what you're talking about" or "You're just trying to confuse me," they are attempting to avoid accountability. This can be particularly damaging as it makes the victim feel like they are overthinking or misremembering situations.

Countering

This involves the narcissist challenging the victim's memory of events, even when the victim remembers them correctly. By saying, "You're wrong, you never remember things correctly," the narcissist implants doubt in the victim's mind. This doubt is then exploited to reshape memories in ways that suit the narcissist's narrative.

Mockery

This tactic is particularly hurtful as it involves demeaning the victim for expressing legitimate feelings and concerns. Laughing at or making fun of someone's experiences or feelings is a way for the narcissist to dismiss the situation's seriousness and establish dominance.

Blocking/Diverting

Instead of addressing the issue at hand, a narcissist might change the subject or bring up an unrelated topic to divert attention from themselves. Phrases like "Let's not talk about my behavior, what about that time when you..." are attempts to deflect from the main issue and draw the victim into defensive mode.

As we explore further, we will unveil the layers beneath these tactics, attempting to discern the true intentions behind gaslighting. We can only fully arm ourselves against such insidious strategies by understanding its roots.

Unveil the True Intent Behind Gaslighting

The pain of gaslighting goes beyond the confusion of conflicting realities; it's the unsettling feeling of betrayal by someone you trusted. The realization that someone could deliberately distort your reality for their own gain was heart-wrenching and enlightening.

As insidious as it sounds, gaslighting is rarely just about

causing pain or confusion for its own sake. Behind these manipulations often lie deeper, more complex motivations.

In my own experiences, I found that an overwhelming need for control drove some gaslighters. In moments when they felt their grip slipping—when I or someone else questioned them or feared exposure of their misdeeds—they'd resort to these tactics to regain the upper hand. By making me doubt myself, they hoped to position themselves as the sole reliable source of "truth" in our relationship.

However, it's essential to recognize that not every gaslighter is the same. The reasons for their behavior can vary widely. Behind the bewildering facade of gaslighting lies a myriad of motivations. At times, it's a desperate act of **self-protection**. A gaslighter, cornered and facing the consequences of their actions, might deny any wrongdoing, even if evidence stands starkly against them. This denial serves as their escape route, a shield against repercussions.

For others, gaslighting becomes a tool for asserting **power**. Dominance in a relationship is maintained by keeping the other person perpetually off balance, constantly doubting themselves and their perceptions. This ensures the gaslighter always has the upper hand, maintaining an unhealthy control of the dynamics.

Then there's **projection**, a tactic where gaslighters accuse others of the very behaviors or intentions they are guilty of. By pointing fingers elsewhere, they skillfully divert attention away from their questionable actions.

In more systematic and societal contexts, gaslighting can be used to **reinforce stereotypes**. We see this, especially in gender dynamics, where women, for instance, might be dismissed as being *hysterical* or *overreacting*. Such tactics have long been employed to invalidate genuine concerns and emotions.

Lastly, some employ gaslighting as a means for an **ego boost**. They derive a perverse sense of accomplishment from seeing their victims question reality. It's a game to them, and every moment of doubt they instill is a point scored in their favor.

Each of these motivations, while distinct, paints a picture of the intricate and often dark tapestry of human behavior and interactions.

As I journeyed through my understanding of these motives, I began to grasp an essential truth. *It wasn't about me.* The distortions and manipulations weren't a reflection of my perceptions but a result of their insecurities and needs. This revelation was both freeing and empowering. While understanding their motives didn't excuse their behavior, it gave me the clarity to approach these situations more assertively.

With this newfound understanding, the next step was reclaiming my emotional ground. This journey was as challenging as it was transformative. The insights from my own experiences and the stories of others who had trodden similar paths became my beacon, guiding me toward a place of strength and self-assurance.

Preparing to Counteract Gaslighting

While trapped in the harrowing maze of gaslighting, the emotional and psychological toll weighed heavily upon me. My very essence seemed under attack. But within this very same darkness, a significant awakening began to unfold. This realization was not just about identifying the tactics of a gaslighter; it was a deep introspection into the profound impact of these tactics on my psyche and many like me.

There was a time when a gust of doubt would consume me. One day, after an exhausting confrontation, I found myself gazing into the mirror, tears streaming down my face. The reflection, looking back, was not one I recognized. The radiant, confident woman I once knew appeared diminished. The individual in that mirror seemed to be crying out for affirmation, craving validation from external sources, and doubting her reality. It was at that very moment that a switch flipped inside me. Was I going to let this external force dictate my self-worth? Was this tormented reflection the legacy I wanted to leave behind?

The days that followed were filled with introspection. I began to journal extensively about the instances when I felt gaslighted and how these instances made me feel. Writing became my sanctuary, a safe space to unpack my emotions without the looming shadow of doubt. Each entry, raw and vulnerable, became a testament to my strength and resilience. On days when doubt would resurface, I would read back through my own words, finding solace and strength in my past revelations.

It wasn't long before I realized that the feelings of inadequacy and doubt, though amplified by gaslighting, had deeper roots. These feelings were intricately tied to long-standing beliefs and experiences from my past, making me more susceptible to the manipulative tactics of gaslighters. It was an epiphany. Understanding the root of my vulnerabilities became the key to strengthening my defenses. By confronting and healing old wounds, I was reclaiming my emotional ground from recent gaslighting attempts and fortifying myself against future ones.

Conversations with fellow empaths became instrumental during this period. Listening to their stories, their moments of realization and awakening, provided me with insights I hadn't considered. It became evident that while our journeys were unique, there were undeniable parallels. One story, in particular, resonated deeply. A friend spoke of how she confronted her gaslighter, armed with evidence and witnesses. The gaslighter's immediate reaction was to deny, divert, and project. But what struck me was her courage in that moment. She had prepared herself, reclaiming her narrative, standing firmly in her truth. The outcome of that confrontation was less about the gaslighter's response and more about her own realization of power and agency.

With every shared story and personal epiphany, the foundation for more advanced coping techniques began to emerge. The overcoming had its pitfalls, but the destination promised empowerment, healing, and transformation. Let's now venture into the real-world implications of gaslighting, where we'll explore and dissect its manifestations in everyday life.

Navigating the Shadows of Gaslighting in Everyday Scenarios

There was that cold evening when I sat across from a dear friend in a cozy café. Between sips of warm cocoa, she shared her experiences with a partner who constantly undermined her memories and feelings. "Maybe I'm just too forgetful," she sighed. Witnessing her questioning her reality was heartbreaking, a classic sign of gaslighting. Drawing from my own experiences and those close to me, I've gathered a set of practical scenarios that might help you navigate this nebulous world.

"You're too sensitive!": After a tense disagreement, the gaslighter might resort to this classic line. They're essentially dismissing your feelings and making you question your emotional responses.

Response:

Rather than doubting yourself, you can reply, "My feelings are valid, and it's important for me to express them." By asserting yourself, you're not just countering the gaslighter but also reassuring your own self.

The Forgotten Anniversary: Imagine it's your anniversary, and your partner forgets. When you bring it up, they insist, "We never celebrated anniversaries! You're imagining things."

Response:

In this case, trust your memories. "I remember celebrating it last year at [specific place]. It's important to me that we acknowledge our milestones."

Constantly Changing Stories: The gaslighter tells you one thing one day and completely denies it the next, leaving you disoriented.

Response:

Maintain a mental or physical note of important conversations. "On [specific date], you mentioned this. It helps me when we have consistent communication."

Discrediting Your Achievements: You share a success at work, and the gaslighter minimizes it by saying, "Anyone could have done that."

Response:

Stay grounded in your worth. "This achievement means a lot to me. I worked hard for it and am proud of what I've accomplished."

Shifting Blame: Whenever there's a mistake, the gaslighter never takes responsibility and somehow makes it your fault.

Response:

Be clear about where responsibility lies. "This situation is not a result of my actions. We need to acknowledge our individual roles."

Navigating through these situations, I've realized that the key is to trust oneself. While gaslighters may cast shadows of doubt, holding onto one's sense of reality becomes the beacon of light. There will be moments when the gaslighter's words echo loudly, tempting us to question our reality. But with each assertive response and affirmation of our truths, we create a protective shield around our mental and emotional well-being.

Remember that you're not alone. Just like me and my friend found our way out of the gaslighting maze, so can you. With awareness, practical strategies, and unwavering self-belief, the fog will eventually clear, revealing the path to genuine, respectful relationships. And as we continue this exploration, we'll also delve into understanding the enigmatic nature of dark empaths, another essential step in shielding ourselves from emotional manipulators.

4

GUARD YOURSELF FROM THE DARK EMPATH

Discover the Dual Nature of the Dark Empath

The world of empaths is truly diverse, just as varied as the human experience itself. Among the mosaic of personalities I've encountered, the Dark Empath remains one of the most intriguing. Their unique blend of empathic sensitivity intertwined with shadowy inclinations sets them apart in the vast realm of human behaviors. Reflecting on my own experiences, I've often found myself drawn into the captivating aura of such individuals, initially mistaking their depth for pure empathic understanding.

The essence of the Dark Empath is the *paradox* they represent. On one hand, they possess a genuine ability to connect with emotions, resonating with feelings and mirroring them in a profoundly real manner. This is the side that pulls you in and makes you believe in the authenticity of the connection. Their capacity to understand and articulate emotions can sometimes surpass even the most genuine empaths. This depth of understanding stems from their intrinsic nature to grasp emotional nuances.

Yet, lurking beneath this surface of empathic resonance is a side less benign. Here, the narcissistic and darker traits intermingle with their empathic tendencies. While they're not driven by malevolence, their motivations are more complex than pure empaths. Their actions and responses are often tinted with a self-serving hue, subtly steering interactions to their advantage.

Recognizing this duality was an eye-opener. It taught me the importance of vigilant awareness, ensuring that while I basked in the depth of connection with a Dark Empath, I remained anchored in reality, safeguarding my emotional well-being.

Discern Overlapping Traits that Make Them Dangerous

In my first encounters with Dark Empaths, I was taken in by their charm. The depth of understanding they showcased and their ability to resonate with my feelings was unlike any other connection I had experienced. We shared intimate conversations, and it felt as though they truly *got* me. However, as the layers unraveled, I began to see behavior patterns that did not align with the empathic traits they initially displayed.

We must delineate the traits that differentiate a Dark Empath from a conventional narcissist. While their behaviors might appear alarmingly similar at first glance, a more nuanced examination reveals subtle (and sometimes not-so-subtle) variations.

At their core, a Dark Empath retains that ability to feel deeply, just as any empath does. They resonate with emotions around them and can tap into the sentiments of others with astonishing precision. This innate sensitivity often makes their manipulations more refined than typical narcissists'. Because they genuinely feel, their manipulations can come from a place of understanding and sometimes even compassion, making it harder to detect and more challenging to resist. It's almost like they have an internal switch, effortlessly transitioning between genuine connection and self-serving maneuverings.

A narcissist, in contrast, typically manipulates from a place of need – be it for admiration, validation, or control. Their actions, driven by this insatiable hunger, often have a more transparent agenda. These actions can be predictable for the trained eye or someone who's experienced the brunt of narcissistic behavior. They lack genuine emotional depth, substituting it instead with a feigned facade.

But the Dark Empath dances on the edges of both worlds. Their manipulations are more profound because they're based on personal needs and a deep understanding of human emotion. This means they can craft their actions to resonate deeply with their target. For instance, while a narcissist might shower you with compliments to receive praise in return, a Dark Empath will do so because they genuinely appreciate you. Still, they might also have an ulterior motive, such as wanting you to trust them or open up to them. The act is genuine, but the intention might be multi-layered.

Another distinguishing trait is their response to criticism or confrontation. While a narcissist might react with overt aggression or a blatant display of hurt pride, a Dark Empath might outwardly acknowledge their mistake, showcasing emotional understanding and remorse. However, beneath that acknowledgment, they might harbor resentment or plot a discreet form of retaliation. This makes them unpredictable, as they can oscillate between genuine empathy and cunning stratagems.

For empaths, this duality presents a complex challenge. Our instinct to connect and heal might pull us towards a Dark Empath, believing that the genuine connection felt can override their shadow side. But it's crucial to remember that just as light and shadow coexist, the balance of their motives can shift. Today's genuine connection might be tomorrow's manipulation.

Engaging with a Dark Empath isn't necessarily a journey of strife. With knowledge and understanding, it can be an expedition of growth, setting clear boundaries, and learning to prioritize oneself. After understanding the nuanced psyche of the Dark Empath, it becomes crucial to recognize how these traits manifest in everyday interactions. Let's dive into real-world scenarios to discern the tactics of narcissists from the often-subtler strategies of dark empaths.

Spotting Dark Empath Behaviors in the Real World

Now that we've touched on their inherent traits, let's transition into the tangible world. Here, we'll identify specific behaviors and tactics of Dark Empaths, differentiating them from the more overt strategies of narcissists.

The Compliment Game:

Narcissist: Compliments are primarily used to gain leverage or as a precursor to a favor. They might say, "You've always been there for me unlike others." Here, they're putting someone else down while elevating you, only to possibly devalue you later.

Dark Empath: Their compliments are more emotion-driven, making them seem sincere. "I sensed you needed some praise today," they might say, subtly reminding you of their emotional insight into your vulnerabilities.

Shared Secrets:

Narcissist: They might share a 'secret' (sometimes fabricated) about someone, making you feel 'special' or 'trusted'—only to use it against you later.

Dark Empath: They'll share a deeply emotional story or secret, binding you closer with threads of shared vulnerabilities, making it hard for you ever to question their intentions or authenticity.

Disagreements:

Narcissist: They tend to rage or give silent treatment when confronted or when they don't get their way.

Dark Empath: They'd employ emotional language, perhaps even tear up, making you feel guilty for bringing up the issue in the first place.

Rescuer vs. Healer:

Narcissist: Positions themselves as the 'rescuer' – reminding you continuously of their 'sacrifices' for you.

Dark Empath: Projects themselves as a 'healer,' saying things like, "I can sense your pain, let me help you through it," making it difficult for you to discern genuine assistance from manipulation.

Emotional Dumps:

Narcissist: Often rants about their day, expecting sympathy and attention, without much regard for your emotions or experiences.

Dark Empath: They engage in an emotional dump but frame it in a way that they were 'reminded of a traumatic past event' or 'feeling your pain.' This makes you feel obligated to comfort them even when you might be the one needing support.

Recalling my interactions with both personalities, I remember the confusion I often felt. An encounter with a friend —she often alluded to her deep understanding of my emotions. Initially, it felt comforting. But as time wore on, our conversations seemed to center around her 'sensing' something amiss with me, even when I felt perfectly fine. She would then dive into her own past traumas, often overshadowing any sentiment I wished to express. It was a perplexing mix of empathy and overshadowing —classic dark empath behavior.

In another instance, a colleague constantly showered me with praises, but there was always a hidden barb. "You're so much more understanding than others," he'd say, subtly pushing me to do more work. His tactics were clear and overt—a classic narcissist.

By comparing and contrasting these behaviors, we empower ourselves to recognize the signs early on. As we delve deeper into this realm, you'll gain tools and strategies to interact with them in a way that preserves your well-being, ensuring that you remain grounded and empowered.

Strategize Against Dark Empath Manipulations

Navigating interactions with a Dark Empath can sometimes feel like traversing a maze with no exit in sight. Recalling my entanglements with such deceptive personalities, each turn I took led me to confusion and self-doubt. Yet, with introspection and resilience, I unearthed strategies that shielded me from their intricate webs. Your journey with a Dark Empath might differ, but the following strategies, derived from my lessons and observations, will offer a starting point to guard your empathic essence.

Introductory Grounding Techniques

In the aftermath of encounters with a Dark Empath, I often found myself emotionally adrift. The importance of grounding cannot be overstated. Simple practices like deep breathing or clutching a physical object were my early tools to regain composure. By grounding, I could fend off the consuming energies of the Dark Empath. We'll delve deeper into more advanced grounding rituals and exercises in Chapter 6, ensuring you're well-prepared for various emotional upheavals.

Reflect, Don't Absorb

I realized the subtle yet profound distinction between acknowledging another's emotions and absorbing them. Creating a mental barrier was my solution. Whenever I felt overwhelmed, I'd halt and introspect, "Is this emotion mine?" This immediate reflection often prevented me from bearing emotions not my own, shielding me from undue stress.

Establish Emotional Boundaries

The allure of a Dark Empath often lies in their knack for weaving into your emotional fabric. Setting clear emotional boundaries was my safeguard. When they'd steer our discussions into unsettling terrains, I mastered the art of voicing my discomfort or subtly changing the course of our conversation. These boundaries were my fortress, ensuring my emotional well-being wasn't jeopardized.

Limited Exposure

With increasing awareness, I realized that prolonged engagements with a Dark Empath drained me. Completely sidestepping them might be unfeasible, especially if they're integral to your personal or professional circle. However, modulating the interaction duration, spacing out meetings, or occasional digital breaks worked wonders for me. I will detail more comprehensive strategies to ward off negative influences in Chapter 9.

Tap into Neutral Feedback

There were instances when I grappled with self-doubt, pondering whether my judgments were clouded. In such moments, seeking perspectives from trusted allies proved enlightening. Their unbiased viewpoints, devoid of emotional ties, provided clarity, helping me discern the reality of my interactions with the Dark Empath.

Trust Your Intuition

The Dark Empath's blend of warmth interspersed with cold can seed self-doubt. In such turbulent moments, my inner mantra echoed: "Trust yourself." Especially as empaths, our intuition is an astute compass. If an interaction feels awry, it probably is. Chapter 9 will guide you in rebuilding and reaffirming this trust, especially after traumatic encounters.

Navigate Away from Power Dynamics

Dark Empaths sometimes indulge in power plays, attempting to dominate the narrative. Sensing such dynamics, I'd tactically disengage. This could mean switching topics, taking a brief hiatus, or even cordially agreeing to disagree. Such maneuvers ensured my emotional tranquility remained intact.

Facing a Dark Empath is undeniably challenging. However, each encounter is a lesson, enhancing your defense mechanisms. It's an ongoing journey of setting and resetting boundaries. With every engagement, you'll find yourself more adept, resilient, and harmoniously in sync with your emotional sphere.

As we journey further, I'll equip you with deeper insights, tools, and strategies, fortifying you against the varied challenges that may cross your path.

5

BREAK AWAY FROM THE GRIP OF CODEPENDENCY

Delving into the Roots and Realities of Codependency

In the relationships I've navigated and witnessed, achieving a balance between independence and interdependence often emerges as a central challenge. While healthy relationships thrive on mutual respect and reciprocity, some veer towards a stifling codependency.

It's noteworthy that codependency frequently finds a companion in narcissism. Narcissists, driven by their profound need for validation and dominance, resonate with those entangled in codependency. In their quest for connection, the codependent might mistake the narcissist's controlling nature as a plea for understanding or support. This dynamic mirrors a moth drawn irresistibly to a flame, where the veneer of vulnerability the narcissist projects ensnares the codependent's inherent compassion.

At its essence, codependency surpasses mere reliance; it's an intense emotional or psychological dependence, often on a partner grappling with issues like illness or addiction. Sometimes, this addiction is the narcissist's unending quest for control. Through introspection and observing others, I've discerned that these bonds often stem less from the needs of our partners and more from our internal voids.

During a particularly vulnerable period in my life, I found myself drawn to a partner who, on the surface, seemed to need my strength and support. I was the *rock*, the *savior*. The initial days felt rewarding, filling me with a sense of purpose. But as time progressed, the relationship began draining me, and instead of mutual support, it became a single-directional flow. Every decision and emotion revolved around this person's needs, leaving my desires and well-being on the backburner.

Reflecting on this chapter of my life, I realized this was not just about helping someone; it was about seeking validation, wanting to be needed, and fearing solitude. Codependency became an intricate dance of intertwined fears and needs. It was a lens through which I viewed my worth, tying my self-value to my ability to support and be indispensable to someone else.

But why do we, especially empaths, sometimes find ourselves in such a dynamic? It often concerns our innate desire to heal, nurture, and connect deeply. Our sensitive nature sometimes misinterprets the need to save someone as a meaningful connection. And while there's beauty in empathy and compassion, it's essential to recognize when it crosses into a realm that's detrimental to our well-being.

I remember seeking advice during this phase, and a wise

friend told me, "In your quest to light up others' worlds, don't let your own light diminish." These words were the catalyst for introspection. I began attending group therapy sessions and read extensively on codependency, seeking to understand and, more importantly, change this pattern.

The deeply personal terrain of my experiences with codependency set me on a quest for deeper comprehension. There's solace in understanding, bridging the chasm between what we feel and what science tells us. We gain a holistic view by connecting the dots between lived experiences and the underlying mechanisms. Armed with insights from my personal journey, I found myself drawn to the science behind codependency. It was time to delve into the intricacies of the mind to uncover what drives such patterns and behaviors.

A Personal Dive into the Science of Codependency

While walking through my own codependency maze, I often pondered the more profound question: *Why?* Why was my mind caught in this loop of seeking validation and fearing solitude? Delving into the science behind it offered some illuminating insights, which I believe can be a beacon for many navigating similar terrains.

Brain Chemistry and its Whims

During my reading escapades on relationships, I stumbled upon some interesting facts about dopamine, our brain's *feel-good* neurotransmitter. When we feel validated or loved, our brain releases this chemical, bathing us in warmth and happiness. It's fascinating, isn't it? Every time I felt indispensable to someone, my brain might have been giving me a dopamine *hig'*. It became a cycle - the more validation I received, the better I felt.

But it wasn't always sunshine. Those moments of feeling dismissed or undervalued? Perhaps my brain's stress circuits were reacting, releasing the hormone cortisol. Those nights, I lay awake fearing the end of a relationship might've been this cortisol playing its tricks.

Childhood Echoes in Adult Choices

While revisiting my past and trying to decipher the origins of my patterns, I encountered the concept of *attachment styles*. These are the emotional blueprints we form during our early years. An anxious attachment style, possibly sprouting from my past experiences, often nudged me towards relationships where I felt *needed*. It was a bittersweet realization; the child within was trying to find a semblance of security in adult bonds.

Similarly, I recognized some cognitive patterns in myself. On introspection, there were times I saw situations as black and white. A disagreement, in my mind, was a catastrophe waiting to unfold. This might've been *catastrophizing*, a cognitive distortion coloring my perceptions.

Marrying Science with Experience

It became clearer how these scientific truths were mirrored in my narrative. The insatiable need to be indispensable, the sleepless nights fearing solitude, they all had roots, not just in personal experiences, but in the very fabric of my being.

Understanding the science behind codependency wasn't a detached academic exercise; it was a profoundly personal journey. It taught me compassion, not just for others but for myself. I felt weight lifting by realizing that codependency wasn't a character flaw but a dance of biology and past experiences. As we progress further, I hope this knowledge serves as a guide, helping us form bonds rooted in genuine connection and mutual growth.

Breaking away from codependency is not about shunning the need to connect or help; it's about understanding our motivations, establishing boundaries, and ensuring we maintain our individuality. Our next step is to zoom into the micro. It's essential to grasp the *why* behind our behaviors and recognize the *what* – the tangible signs and symptoms that hint at underlying codependent patterns. With a foundation of understanding in place, we are better equipped to discern these indicators and, subsequently, chart a path toward healthier relational dynamics. Let's embark on this discovery of recognition and introspection.

Recognize and Address Symptoms of Codependency

Codependency can be incredibly subtle, sneaking into relationships without either party recognizing it. My very first brush with it was in a close friendship. I constantly prioritized her needs above mine, believing her happiness was my responsibility. Over time, I felt exhausted, emotionally spent, and somewhat lost. It was like I was living two lives, mine and hers, but without truly enjoying either.

But how do you truly discern if what you're experiencing is genuine concern for someone or the chains of codependency tightening around you?

For me, the initial signs were a persistent feeling of **exhaustion.** I was always tired, not from physical exertion, but from the mental and emotional toll of constantly managing, or in some cases, micro-managing another person's life. There were endless nights I lay awake, worrying about her problems, brainstorming solutions, and strategizing ways to 'fix' everything for them.

Another telltale sign was the onset of **resentment**. Even as I went above and beyond to cater to her needs, a small part of me began to feel unseen and unappreciated. I wondered, "When is it my turn? When do my feelings and needs get prioritized?" Initially just a spark, this resentment soon became a blazing fire, affecting our interactions and the relationship's overall health.

Furthermore, I realized I had developed a crippling **fear of rejection or abandonment**. Every disagreement or conflict felt like a potential end, leading to desperate measures to appease and avoid any form of confrontation.

However, the real turning point was when I no longer recognized the person staring back at me in the mirror. My goals, dreams, desires – everything seemed hazy, distant, or aligned with theirs. My identity was overshadowed by theirs, and my self-worth was tightly knit with their approval or validation.

For instance, I started by penning down my thoughts and feelings to see patterns and assess the weight I was placing on myself to *solve other* problems. It provided an avenue for self-reflection, allowing me to reassess and reframe my perspective on my role in others' lives. Then, I arranged a heart-to-heart with my friend, expressing my feelings and concerns. While it was tough, this candid conversation paved the way for a healthier dynamic. It was a lesson in the importance of voicing my needs and ensuring mutual respect in any relationship.

Recognizing the symptoms of codependency was the initial, crucial step in my journey to freedom. It required introspection, courage, and a deep commitment to self-care. Throughout this process, I had to be vigilant, ensuring I didn't revert to old habits.

True independence and self-worth aren't about grand transformations but small, consistent choices—when you prioritize yourself, affirm your value, set boundaries, and rediscover long-lost passions. Each decision draws you nearer to your true, radiant self.

Understanding codependency is vital, but applying this knowledge to real-life situations is where true change happens. Think of it as learning the theory of swimming and then finally diving into the pool. Now, let's explore some hands-on scenarios to navigate moments when codependency looms large.

Overcoming Codependency in Real-Life Situations

Navigating the nuances of codependency can often feel like a walk through a maze, with its complexities and potential pitfalls. I've wandered those pathways where the lines blurred between helping and becoming overly entangled. Through my own experiences, I've unearthed actionable insights. So, let's discover together real-life scenarios—moments that might mirror instances from your life or the lives of those around you. By exploring these situations, I hope to offer both a map and a compass to guide you toward healthier relational dynamics, drawing from well-researched strategies and lessons my experiences have taught me.

Scenario: Friend in Constant Crisis

Your friend seems to be in perpetual distress, from financial woes to relationship struggles, and you're always the first call. While it's okay to be a shoulder to lean on, a codependent bond can form if this becomes one-sided and draining.

Actionable Step: Instead of offering immediate solutions or jumping into rescue mode, ask guiding questions that empower them to think critically and find solutions. For example, "What do you think would be the best step forward?" or "How have you handled similar situations in the past?"

Scenario: Partner's Emotional Well-being Dictates Yours

Every time your partner is upset, you find your mood plummeting too. You may even sideline your feelings or needs to prioritize theirs.

Actionable Step: Create a self-care routine that's separate from your partner's moods. For instance, if you love morning walks, continue that routine even if your partner had a rough night. This ensures you have a semblance of emotional independence.

Scenario: Taking Over Responsibilities

You find yourself always picking up the slack, be it finishing up chores, paying bills, or making all the decisions in a group setting.

Actionable Step: Start small. Designate a day or task where others are responsible. For instance, if you always cook, ask your partner or roommate to take over for one night. It might be uncomfortable at first, but it establishes a precedent.

Scenario: Fear of Conflict

You avoid any confrontation, fearing it might lead to abandonment or escalate into a bigger fight. Thus, you often acquiesce, even when you disagree.

Actionable Step: Begin with non-threatening topics. Practice expressing your opinions on mundane things like movie choices or dinner spots. Gradually, you'll build the confidence to voice more significant concerns.

Scenario: Constant Need for Validation

You send a message, and if there's no immediate reply, you fret, wondering if you said something wrong. You're always looking for affirmation from others to feel good.

Actionable Step: Every time you seek external validation, pause and ask yourself, "Why do I need this? What am I feeling?" Then, self-validate. For instance, if you're proud of a project, acknowledge that pride internally without waiting for others to applaud.

Scenario: Difficulty Saying "No"

Every time someone asks for a favor, you say yes, stretching yourself thin, irrespective of your bandwidth.

Actionable Step: Practice declining small requests that you genuinely can't accommodate. It can be as simple as, "I'm sorry, I can't make it tonight. Let's reschedule." The more you practice, the easier it will become.

Scenario: Merging Identities in a Relationship

You find your hobbies, interests, and even your future goals becoming eerily similar to your partner's while your original aspirations take a backseat.

Actionable Step: Dedicate time for yourself each week to do something you love or explore a new hobby. This 'me-time' is crucial to maintain your unique identity.

While every situation is unique, the underlying principle remains consistent: gradually recognizing patterns and implementing changes. By discerning these tendencies and grasping their impact, you initiate a journey towards healing and embracing your true, independent self. In the chapters ahead, we'll explore how to harness our vulnerabilities, transforming them into powerful assets that help us navigate relationships and empower us in every facet of our lives.

Healing and self-improvement require active dedication. It's a deliberate daily choice, pushing forward even when challenges arise. This commitment paves the way to an authentic life, rich with purpose and inner tranquility.

6

———

TRANSFORM VULNERABILITY INTO PERSONAL STRENGTH

Turn Your Vulnerabilities into Powerhouses

Throughout our shared journey of self-awareness and empowerment, I've realized a pivotal truth that might resonate with you, too: our vulnerabilities, which often seem like hindrances, can be our most potent sources of strength.

You and I, as empaths, experience the world deeply, feeling emotions on a level many might not comprehend. While beautiful in their depth, these heightened sensitivities can sometimes leave us feeling exposed or overwhelmed. I've been there, feeling like my vulnerabilities were my Achilles' heel, especially when faced with negative energies or manipulative personalities.

However, with introspection and experience, I've learned that these so-called *weaknesses* can be transformed into powerhouses of resilience and empowerment.

You initiate an internal shift when you truly recognize and embrace your vulnerabilities. This self-awareness is a brave step forward. By accepting these parts of yourself, you can devise strategies to manage and even harness them.

Think about the deep emotional connections you form. Yes, they might make you susceptible to pain, but also open up realms of joy, love, and fulfillment that many might never know. This emotional depth is a gift, offering you unparalleled insights and bonds. By cherishing this aspect of yourself, you're not just understanding emotions but living them deeply and profoundly.

Another trait we often grapple with is absorbing the emotions around us, leading sometimes to emotional drain. I've felt this weight many times. But with a shift in perspective, I've realized that this absorption is a testament to our profound connection ability. With the right boundaries, you can channel this skill to heal others and better understand and care for yourself.

Transforming vulnerabilities isn't about suppression or denial. It's about acknowledging them, understanding their power, and then channeling them effectively. I promise you once you start seeing them in this new light, you'll realize that these are not just vulnerabilities but unique strengths that set you apart.

As we continue our exploration, I'll guide you on how to ground these sensitivities, ensuring they become your pillars of strength. Remember, it's all about balance – owning your vulnerabilities without letting them overshadow your immense potential.

Techniques and Strategies for Emotional Grounding

While entrenched in self-awareness and acceptance, empowerment requires actionable steps to anchor oneself amidst life's emotional tempests. The next step in our journey together is *grounding*: for us empaths, it is comparable to the roots of a tree. Just as a tree uses its roots to draw nutrients and stabilize itself, we can use grounding to center our emotions and protect ourselves from overwhelming driving forces. And trust me, in a world brimming with different energies, especially when dealing with challenging personalities like narcissists, having a grounding routine can be a lifesaver.

Deep Breathing

The simplest strategies often prove the most effective; they became my immediate go-to during emotionally charged situations. By taking a few moments to breathe deeply, I not only provided my brain with an extra dose of oxygen but also created a brief pause, allowing me to respond instead of reacting impulsively. This technique was beneficial in diffusing the immediate impact of a narcissist's attempt to trigger or provoke.

Trigger: Emotional escalation or feeling worn out.

Insight: When faced with a sudden onslaught of emotions, our instinctual fight or flight response can kick in. Deep breathing calms this response, allowing clearer thinking and more measured reactions.

Practical Tip: Try the 4-7-8 technique: Breathe in for 4 counts, hold for 7 counts, and exhale for 8 counts. Repeat this at least three times. Compared to inhale, the extended exhale helps calm the nervous system.

Visualization

Visualization served as a refuge. When interactions became unbearable, I'd visualize a protective bubble or shield around me, keeping the negative energies at bay. This gave me a psychological edge and reinforced my belief in my inner strength and resilience.

Trigger: Sensing external negative energies or feeling emotionally invaded.

Insight: Visualization uses the power of the mind to create mental barriers against external negativity, reinforcing one's personal space.

Practical Tip: Envision a radiant energy field surrounding you. Imagine this field as impenetrable, where negative energies simply bounce off, leaving you untouched and serene inside.

Rooting Technique

The Rooting Technique became my solace during the most tumultuous times, especially when I was battling the overpowering energies of narcissists. This visualization exercise reconnected me to the Earth, reminding me of my strength and stability, even when external forces attempted to shake my foundation.

Trigger: Feeling emotionally adrift or overwhelmed by the energies of others.

Insight: The Rooting Technique offers a mental anchor, drawing strength from the Earth and reminding you of your innate stability and power. This visualization instills a profound sense of connectedness with the Earth and your innermost self.

Practical Tip: Begin by standing or sitting comfortably. Close your eyes and take a deep, calming breath. Visualize roots emerging from the soles of your feet, diving deep into the Earth, penetrating layers of soil and stone. Feel the energy of the Earth rising, flowing up through these roots, filling your body with a warm, golden light. As this energy envelops you, let it wash away any overwhelming emotions or negative energies. Once you feel centered and grounded, slowly retract the roots back into your feet and open your eyes, carrying with you the renewed energy and sense of stability.

Physical Grounding

Grounding exercises, like feeling the texture of an object, stamping feet, or clenching and unclenching hands, became invaluable tools. These actions reminded me of the present moment and allowed me to detach from any overpowering emotion the narcissist might be trying to induce. They served as physical anchors, reminding me of my agency and presence.

Trigger: Feeling mentally disconnected or overly absorbed in emotions.

Insight: Grounding exercises provide a physical anchor to the present, diverting attention from swirling emotions to tangible sensations.

Practical Tip: A helpful technique is the "5-4-3-2-1" method. Identify five things you can see, four you can touch, three you can hear, two you can smell, and one you can taste. This redirects your focus and grounds you inside the moment.

Mindfulness Meditation

Integrating mindfulness into my daily routine transformed my emotional landscape. It enhanced my self-awareness, enabling me to detect and address emotional disturbances before they intensified. By observing my thoughts and emotions without judgment, I could discern the underlying patterns, anticipate potential triggers, and equip myself to handle them better.

Trigger: Overthinking or ruminating about past/future events.

Insight: Mindfulness cultivates a non-judgmental awareness of the present, preventing the mind from getting caught in distressing loops.

Practical Tip: Start with just five minutes daily. Sit comfortably, close your eyes, and focus on your breathing. If your mind wanders, gently bring it back without judgment.

Nature Retreats

Nature, in itself, has been a profound grounding force for me. Whether it's the rhythmic sounds of waves crashing against the shore, the rustling of leaves, or simply feeling the grass under my feet – these experiences bring a sense of peace and connection to the present moment. If you haven't tried it yet, take some time to immerse yourself in nature. Feel its calming embrace, and let it guide you back to your center.

Trigger: Feeling claustrophobic, trapped in urban stimuli.

Insight: Nature's vastness and tranquility serve as an antidote to the hustle and chaos of daily life, offering perspective and solace.

Practical Tip: Dedicate at least one day a month for a nature retreat. If you're urban-bound, even a quiet hour in a park, focusing on the rustle of leaves or the play of sunlight, can be rejuvenating.

Journaling

As mentioned before, journaling became a lifesaver for me, particularly when the weight of my emotions felt too heavy to bear alone. It provided a safe space to pour out my feelings, the intricacies of my interactions with narcissists, and my reflections on the dance between empathy and narcissism.

Trigger: Overwhelming emotions, confusion, or needing clarity regarding a particular situation or relationship.

Insight: Journaling acts as a mirror to your soul. By penning down your feelings, you're releasing pent-up emotions and gaining clarity by seeing things from an external perspective. It offers a tangible means to track patterns, growth, and progress, clearly showing your journey and how far you've come.

Practical Tip: Start by setting aside a few quiet minutes daily, just for yourself. Choose a medium that feels right – be it a traditional diary, a digital journal, or even voice memos. Begin writing without overthinking. Let your emotions, thoughts, and memories flow. If you find it challenging to start, try using prompts like: "Today I felt...", "A situation that puzzled me today was...", or "Something I learned about myself today...". Over time, you'll notice that journaling doesn't just chronicle your experiences but also aids in healing and self-awareness.

Setting Boundaries

Often, the invisible lines we draw hold the most significant impact. Setting boundaries became a pivotal tool in my journey as an empath. By clearly defining what I was comfortable with emotionally and physically, I ensured that my interactions remained respectful and enriching. This technique was especially crucial in interactions with narcissists, preventing them from taking undue advantage of my empathic nature.

Trigger: Feeling exhausted, excessively drained, or sensing a violation of personal space and emotions.

Insight: Boundaries act as a protective shield, safeguarding an empath's emotional and energetic space. They help in delineating personal limits, ensuring that you don't lose yourself in the vast ocean of external emotions, especially when dealing with those who have narcissistic tendencies.

Practical Tip: Begin by identifying your non-negotiables. If a particular behavior or topic makes you uncomfortable, voice it out. For instance, if a friend frequently delves into negative discussions, you might say, "I value our conversations, but I'd prefer to discuss more uplifting topics. It helps me maintain a positive mindset." This approach is not about shutting people out but ensuring mutually beneficial and respectful interactions.

These techniques helped me maintain my emotional equilibrium during challenging interactions with narcissists and enriched my growth journey. They weren't just defensive strategies; they were tools for empowerment, enabling me to reclaim my space, voice, and agency in the face of manipulation.

Now, as we venture deeper into understanding our empathic nature, I want you to remember the importance of grounding. It's our defense, our sanctuary. When faced with intense emotions or challenging situations, having grounding techniques up your sleeve will empower you to navigate with grace and resilience. And believe me, as we move forward, building resilience is a journey you and I will embark on together, ensuring that your empathic nature remains a strength, not a burden.

Embrace the Power of Self-Compassion

The art of grounding provides a robust shield against external emotional onslaughts, especially from interactions laden with narcissistic undertones. But what happens when the storms aren't external but brewing inside us? The battles within often require a different kind of resilience — a nurturing, tender touch, which I found through the transformative power of self-compassion.

In my journey, when the dust of external confrontations

settled, I was frequently left grappling with internal critics, a slew of *should haves* and *could haves*. Those moments of self-doubt and self-judgment were as daunting as any narcissistic encounter. This was where self-compassion stepped in as a beacon of healing and self-empowerment.

The Healing Touch of Self-compassion

Self-compassion is akin to extending the same kindness, understanding, and patience to oneself that one would offer a dear friend. It's a recognition that flaws, mistakes, and imperfections are part of the shared human experience. When I embraced this perspective, it became easier to navigate moments of personal shortcomings without spiraling into self-criticism.

It's essential, however, to differentiate self-compassion from self-pity. While the latter might overemphasize personal struggles, viewing oneself as a helpless victim, genuine self-compassion transcends self-centeredness. It acknowledges pain and shortcomings but situates them within the broader human experience. Instead of "Why is this happening to me?" the self-compassionate voice gently proclaims, "It's okay, everyone struggles, and I'm not alone."

Cultivating a Self-compassionate Mindset

Embracing self-compassion isn't about suppressing emotions or pasting a happy veneer over pain. It's about acknowledging, cradling, and navigating emotions gracefully. Here are some practices that significantly bolstered my self-compassionate stance:

Self-compassion Affirmations: On days when I felt particularly low or critical of myself, I'd repeat affirmations like, "I am deserving of love and kindness," or "It's okay to have flaws; they don't define my worth." Over time, these phrases became automatic responses to self-judgment, neutralizing its sting.

Comforting Self-touch: Physical gestures, like placing a hand over the heart or hugging oneself, can invoke feelings of warmth, safety, and love. I frequently used these gestures, especially during moments of intense emotional distress. They served as a physical manifestation of self-kindness.

Mindful Journaling: We've previously explored the benefits of journaling for emotional clarity. But, by introducing a self-compassionate lens to it, it morphs into a therapeutic exercise. Begin with writing about a challenging event, then reframe it from a stance of self-kindness and understanding. Remember, the aim isn't to avoid responsibility but to address oneself with the same gentleness one would offer a loved one. Over time, this practice fosters self-compassion and provides greater emotional clarity.

Walking this path, I've realized that self-compassion is a vital companion for empaths, especially when navigating the challenging terrains of narcissistic interactions. As we delve deeper, weaving self-compassion into our daily practices ensures that while we're kind and open to the world, we don't neglect the one person who needs our love the most — ourselves.

So, as we move ahead, I invite you to cradle your vulnerabilities with tenderness, for in that gentle embrace lies an unfathomable strength. This strength will shield you from external adversities and light your path forward, ensuring your journey remains as enriching as it is enlightening.

Join Empath Communities for Support

One of the most enlightening moments in my journey was

when I realized I wasn't alone. Although our empathic experiences are deeply personal, an overarching narrative connects us. Finding and connecting with like-minded individuals who share and understand your experiences can offer both comfort and empowerment.

I remember the first time I stumbled upon an empath community online. Until then, I felt like a lone ship navigating through stormy seas, with only my compass of self-awareness and grounding techniques to guide me. But as I scrolled through stories, experiences, and advice shared by fellow empaths, it felt like finding a harbor. In this safe haven, my ship could anchor and refuel.

Sharing your journey with others who *get it* provides emotional validation and introduces that every empath's journey is unique. By pooling our collective wisdom, we can uncover a reservoir of tools and techniques to benefit us all.

The Power of Shared Stories

Stories have always been a powerful tool for connection. Reading about someone else's encounters, especially those that echoed my own experiences, created a sense of belonging. It affirmed that I wasn't an anomaly but part of a broader tapestry of souls who felt the world deeply. These shared stories also offered insights into how others navigated their challenges, giving me new strategies and tools to consider.

The Benefits of Empathic Exchange

Beyond the stories, there was the power of empathic exchange. Within these communities, we empaths can offer support without the fear of draining ourselves because there's an inherent understanding of energy balance. We uplift each other, celebrate each other's victories, and provide a shoulder when the weight gets too heavy. It's a mutual exchange where the very act of giving also replenishes.

Diverse Perspectives, One Goal

What intrigued me the most was the diversity within these communities. From different walks of life, cultures, and experiences, we all converged with a shared goal: to thrive in our empathic nature. The diversity meant that there were myriad ways to tackle similar challenges. What worked for one might not work for another, but the vast array of options meant there was always something new to try, a fresh approach to consider.

Where and How to Find Your Tribe

Empath communities flourish both online and offline. There are numerous avenues to explore, from dedicated forums and social media groups to local meetups and workshops. If you're hesitant about diving straight in, start by observing. Lurk in online groups, read conversations, and get a feel of the community. When you're ready, introduce yourself, share a story, or ask a question. You'll be surprised at the warmth and acceptance that awaits.

And if you don't find a community that resonates with you, why not create one? Sometimes, the tribe we seek is waiting for someone to light the beacon and gather them.

Moving Forward Together

It's vital to remember that we don't have to walk alone. The path might be challenging, but we're a formidable force together. Harness the power of community. Let it be your sounding board, your support system, and a reminder of the incredible strength that lies in our collective empathy.

After all, in the words of an African proverb I hold dear, "If you want to go fast, go alone. If you want to go far, go together." While the camaraderie and understanding of these groups offer solace, they also pave the way for a more profound, transformative journey. To fully harness the potential of these revelations, it becomes imperative to cultivate a growth and self-improvement mindset. Embracing this mindset is the key to transforming challenges into stepping stones, ensuring that we don't just cope but continually evolve and thrive.

Cultivate a Growth and Self-Improvement Mindset

Over time, I've recognized that merely navigating my high sensitivities wasn't enough; to truly thrive, it was essential to evolve continuously. At the heart of this evolution lay the powerful principle of a growth and self-improvement mindset.

Understanding the very essence of this mindset was my first step. Instead of viewing challenges as insurmountable hurdles, I began to perceive them as opportunities for learning and self-expansion. Each interaction became a lesson, especially those with energy-draining individuals like narcissists. Instead of asking, "Why is this happening to me?" I shifted to "What can I learn from this?" However, everything changed when I decided to view my emotional landscape not as a hindrance but as a tool for self-improvement. I want to share with you this transformative shift, emphasizing the beauty of continuous learning and evolution.

Becoming an Active Architect of Your Life

A fixed mindset often leaves us feeling trapped in our circumstances. However, embracing a growth perspective allowed me to reclaim agency in my life. It became clear that while I couldn't control every external event, I had complete authority over my reactions and growth. This shift was transformative. No longer was I a passive recipient of life's experiences; I became an active participant, constantly seeking ways to refine my understanding, responses, and emotional health.

The Ripple Effects of Continuous Learning

Committing to self-improvement wasn't just about handling the present better and equipping myself for the future. I delved into books, courses, and seminars that focused on empathy, emotional intelligence, and personal development. As my knowledge reservoir expanded, I found myself better prepared to handle newer challenges. What previously felt overwhelming started to become manageable, even surmountable, with the tools and strategies I'd equipped myself with.

Embracing Change and Adaptability

One of the hallmarks of a growth mindset is adaptability. As empaths, the emotional landscapes we navigate are ever-changing. What helped me yesterday might not be as effective today. Recognizing this fluidity, I learned to be flexible in my approaches. This adaptability ensured I wasn't rigidly stuck in old patterns but constantly evolving in my empathic journey.

Seeking Feedback as a Catalyst for Growth

In the realm of personal development, feedback became invaluable. Instead of shying away, I actively sought it, especially from trusted friends and my empath community. Understanding how others perceived my reactions and strategies gave me fresh perspectives, highlighting areas of improvement I hadn't considered.

As this growth and self-improvement evolution unfolded, my

transformation wasn't just internal. The external facets of my life began to mirror this growth. My relationships deepened, my professional life flourished, and, most importantly, my bond with myself became fortified.

With this fortified mindset and the continuous commitment to self-improvement, the path ahead leads to harnessing daily habits that further nurture our emotional and mental well-being. Implementing structured routines and practices ensures that our growth isn't sporadic but consistent, allowing us to navigate the challenges of being an empath and genuinely thrive amidst them.

7

______

ESTABLISH DAILY HABITS FOR YOUR WELL-BEING

Form Habits for Emotional Health

The pathway to well-being, especially for empaths like us, often requires more than a fleeting attempt at self-care. It calls for a deep-rooted commitment, best manifested through consistently practiced habits. These habits are anchors in our lives, ensuring our emotional health remains robust, even when the external environment is tumultuous.

The Foundation of Emotional Health

You might wonder, why focus so intently on habit formation for emotional health? The reason is simple yet profound. Just as our bodies need consistent nourishment through a balanced diet and regular exercise, our emotional selves require daily care and attention. This daily regimen ensures that our emotional reservoirs remain full, allowing us to engage with the world, including the energy-consuming interactions with narcissists, without getting drained.

The Role of Habitual Routine

A structured routine has been my sanctuary. By allocating specific times for reflection, relaxation, and recreation, I ensured that my days had a balanced rhythm. This predictability acted as a buffer against unexpected emotional surges, making me feel more in control and grounded. It's like charting a course through a storm; the established habits become the guiding stars, ensuring we don't lose our way.

The Compound Effect

What's beautiful about these habits is their compound effect over time. Initially, the changes might seem minimal, almost imperceptible. But as days turn into weeks and weeks into months, the positive impact of these habits becomes evident. This isn't about a quick fix but a long-term investment in your emotional well-being.

Integration into Daily Life

Incorporating habits for emotional health doesn't necessarily mean adding more tasks to our already packed schedules. Instead, it's about integrating these practices into our daily routines. It could be as simple as starting the day with a gratitude journal, setting aside ten minutes for meditation, or ensuring we have quality *me-time* amidst our busy lives. Over time, these integrated habits become second nature, a seamless part of our daily lives.

Having recognized the profound impact of consistently practiced habits on my emotional health, I felt compelled to share this with fellow empaths. It's not just about surviving but thriving, even amidst the complexities of our emotional landscapes. As we delve deeper into this chapter, we'll explore tailored tactics you can weave into your daily routine.

As I share these strategies with you, know that they have been thoughtfully crafted to be both insightful and actionable. I've distilled the essence of each approach into a practical composition, removing any ambiguity. This way, you won't find yourself lost in theory but will have clear, straight-to-the-point suggestions to implement. Every tactic is designed with your journey in mind, offering direct guidance to integrate into your daily life, ensuring that every step you take is one towards enhanced emotional resilience and well-being. And remember, it's not just about what you do but *how consistently* you do it. This consistency paves the way for lasting emotional well-being, setting the stage for the next phase of self-care.

Care for Yourself Daily

For empaths, self-care isn't a luxury—it's essential. We need tools to help us manage and preserve our energy, ensuring we don't feel depleted at the end of each day. Daily self-care practices act as mini rejuvenation sessions, helping us regain balance and remain centered. Here's how you can infuse actionable self-care practices into your daily routine.

Start with Mindful Mornings: Before the day's hustle takes over, gift yourself a few moments of tranquility. This could be through a simple meditation practice or a gentle stretching routine. This early morning ritual sets the tone for the day, ensuring you start with a calm and centered mind.

Actionable Tip: Set your alarm ten minutes earlier than usual.

Use this time to practice deep breathing exercises, focusing on each inhale and exhale.

Curate a Nourishing Diet: What we consume directly affects our emotional well-being. As empaths, choosing foods that elevate our mood and energy is essential. Opt for a balanced diet with plenty of fresh fruits, vegetables, and whole grains.

Actionable Tip: Begin your day with a glass of warm lemon water to detoxify and a healthy breakfast like oatmeal topped with fruits and nuts to sustain your energy levels.

Create Empath-Friendly Spaces: Your immediate environment determines your emotional state. Keep your living and working spaces decluttered. Introduce elements like plants, soothing colors, and gentle lighting.

Actionable Tip: Dedicate a corner of your room for relaxation. Add a comfortable chair, a soft throw blanket, a few of your favorite books, and perhaps a diffuser with calming essential oils.

Digital Detox: In this age of constant connectivity, it's essential for empaths to disconnect periodically. This doesn't mean shunning technology but using it mindfully.

Actionable Tip: Establish a 'digital sunset'—an hour before your bedtime, switch off all electronic devices, allowing your mind to transition into a restful state.

Practice Active Listening to Yourself: As empaths, we excel at listening to others, but it's equally crucial to listen to oneself. Throughout the day, check in with yourself. How are you feeling? Are there any emotions you need to address?

Actionable Tip: Set periodic reminders on your phone, prompting you to pause and assess your emotional state.

Engage in Joyful Activities: Immerse in at least one activity daily that brings you genuine joy, whether it's reading, painting, dancing, or even taking a walk in nature. This is not about productivity but pure, unadulterated joy.

Actionable Tip: List five activities that always lift your spirits. Ensure you pick at least one from the list daily.

Connect, But Also Protect: As empaths, it's in our nature to connect deeply. But it's also essential to protect our energies. *Actionable Tip*: Visualize a protective energy bubble around you, especially when you're about to enter potentially draining situations. This mental imagery acts as a shield, helping you maintain your energetic balance.

By incorporating these practices into your daily routine, you're safeguarding your emotional well-being and ensuring you can harness your empathic abilities' full potential. These consistent acts of self-care will serve as a foundation, preparing you for deeper rejuvenation sessions, which we'll delve into as we progress. Remember, every day offers a fresh start, and with these tools at your disposal, you're well-equipped to make the most of it.

Regularly Recharge and Refuel

The rhythm of life can be relentless. While daily self-care is pivotal, there comes a time when every empath needs to delve deeper, taking an intentional pause to recharge and refuel truly. Think of it as a soulful pit-stop, where you replenish what's been expended and stock up for the journey ahead.

Prioritize Periodic Retreats: The world brims with its cacophonies, often drowning out our inner whispers. Periodically retreating from this external noise helps us tune into our own rhythm. This doesn't necessitate a lavish vacation; it can be a quiet weekend at home or a day spent in nature.

Actionable Tip: Schedule a 'me-day' once a month. During this day, focus solely on activities that rejuvenate you. It might be reading, painting, or perhaps a silent walk in the woods.

Harness the Power of Silence: There's a therapeutic quality to silence, an elegance and clarity often overshadowed in our bustling lives. Embrace moments of stillness.

Actionable Tip: Dedicate a few minutes every day to sit in absolute silence. Do nothing. Just be. Feel the weight of your body, the rhythm of your breath, and the gentle flutter of your thoughts.

Deep Sleep—The Ultimate Recharger: Quality sleep is a non-negotiable for empaths. It's the time our body and mind process, heal, and reset.

Actionable Tip: Create a bedtime routine. This might involve dimming the lights, reading a calming book, or practicing a short meditation to ensure a deep, restorative sleep.

Water—Nature's Balm: Water is therapeutically cleansing. Whether it's a warm bath infused with essential oils or a serene walk beside a lake, water has a unique way of washing away emotional residue.

Actionable Tip: When feeling particularly overwhelmed, try a salt bath. Epsom salt, renowned for its grounding properties, can help detox both the body and mind.

Journaling—Dialogues with the Self: I will never tire of stating that transferring thoughts onto paper is a potent way of decluttering the mind. Journaling is less about recording events and more about understanding feelings.

Actionable Tip: Begin with just five minutes of free writing every morning or night. Don't edit or judge; let your thoughts flow, and you'll soon find clarity emerging from the chaos.

Energizing Through Movement: Physical activity, whether it's a structured gym session or an impromptu dance in your living room, releases endorphins, the body's natural mood elevators. *Actionable Tip*: Find a form of movement you genuinely enjoy. It could be yoga, tai chi, or even a brisk walk. Commit to it at least thrice a week.

Regularly immersing ourselves in these rejuvenation rituals ensures our emotional reservoirs remain full. As empaths, we have a profound gift, but it's essential to remember that to give to others, we first need to give to ourselves. By recharging and refueling regularly, we prepare ourselves for the challenges and joys of life, ensuring our empathic journey is sustainable and deeply enriching. And, as we continue this voyage, it's equally vital to harness that renewed vigor in productive ways; hence, the next essential step is to conquer procrastination and maintain unwavering consistency in your actions.

Conquer Procrastination and Stay Consistent

Procrastination, that sly whisperer, often beckons us away from our best intentions. It convinces us that there's always a tomorrow, a later, or a soon. For empaths, battling procrastination is doubly challenging. Our acute sensitivity to energies and emotions means we sometimes delay or avoid tasks that could potentially stir emotional unrest or discomfort.

However, triumph over procrastination is pivotal for self-care and emotional well-being. Let's explore strategies to overcome it, ensuring that you set and follow through with intentions and actions.

Understanding the *Why*: Before diving into solutions, it's essential to grasp the underlying causes of your procrastination. Is it fear of failure, perfectionism, or perhaps the task evokes unsettling emotions? Recognizing the root cause can be a game-changer.

Actionable Tip: When you feel the urge to delay a task, pause and introspect. Ask yourself, "Why am I avoiding this?" Please write down the reasons and confront them.

Break Tasks into Manageable Bites: Often, procrastination results from feeling overwhelmed. The task at hand seems huge, and we delay starting it.

Actionable Tip: Break down tasks into smaller, more achievable steps. Instead of "I will meditate for an hour," begin with "I will meditate for five minutes today." Small victories pave the way for bigger triumphs.

Set Specific Deadlines: Open-ended tasks tend to be pushed into the infinite abyss of 'someday'.

Actionable Tip: Assign deadlines to your tasks. If you aim to incorporate a daily self-care ritual, set a start date. Having a clear timeline fosters accountability.

Employ the Two-minute Rule: If a task takes less than two minutes, do it immediately. This rule, simple in its essence, can profoundly reduce the clutter of pending tasks.

Actionable Tip: Reply to that email now. Wash that cup right after your coffee. Small tasks often accumulate and become overwhelming; tackle them promptly.

Visualize the End Result: Envisioning the outcome can be a powerful motivator.

Actionable Tip: Before starting a task, close your eyes and imagine its successful completion. How do you feel? Relieved? Joyful? Harness those emotions as fuel.

Accountability Partnerships: Share your goals with someone trustworthy. Knowing that someone else is aware of your intentions can instill a sense of responsibility.

Actionable Tip: Partner with a friend and share daily or weekly goals. Check in on each other's progress and celebrate milestones together.

Forgive and Restart: There will be days when procrastination wins, and that's okay. Beating yourself up only creates negative energy. *Actionable Tip*: If you falter, acknowledge it without judgment. Offer yourself forgiveness and start anew the next day.

Consistency, born from conquering procrastination, isn't just about ticking off tasks. It's about creating a rhythm, a harmony in our lives where self-care becomes second nature, not an afterthought. Remember, each day is an opportunity, a blank slate. Letting procrastination cloud it or paint it with purposeful action is in our hands. As we venture further, we'll explore ways to reinforce these positive habits, ensuring their formation and sustenance to guarantee continued success on this empathic journey.

Reinforce Habits for Continued Success

Building a habit is much like planting a seed; it requires patience, nurturing, and constant attention. However, the real challenge begins not at the inception but in sustaining the growth. As empaths, establishing well-being habits goes beyond mere self-care; it's about creating an ecosystem where we can flourish emotionally and mentally.

Visualize Long-term Gains: While the immediate benefits of a habit can be motivating, the long-term gains offer sustained drive. For instance, meditation might offer immediate relaxation. Still, its long-term advantages—enhanced clarity, emotional balance, and improved focus—are the real treasures.

Actionable Tip: Create a vision board or maintain a journal detailing the long-term advantages of your habits. Refer to it during moments of wavering motivation.

Track Your Progress: Monitoring your journey provides tangible evidence of your commitment and progress. It's motivating to see how far you've come.

Actionable Tip: Use habit-tracking apps or a simple calendar. Mark days when you successfully follow through with your habits. Over time, you'll want to keep the streak going.

Establish Rituals: A ritual is a habit imbued with intent and mindfulness. For empaths, rituals can be especially grounding. Instead of mechanically journaling every day, make it a ritual. Light a candle, play calming music, and then write down your thoughts.

Actionable Tip: Infuse habits with a sense of purpose and ceremony. The added layer of significance makes them more engaging.

Engage in Periodic Reviews: Taking time to assess your progress helps realign your actions with goals. Maybe a habit needs tweaking, or perhaps it's no longer serving its purpose.

Actionable Tip: Set aside a day every month for a habit review. Reflect on what's working and what's not, and adjust accordingly.

Reward Yourself: Positive reinforcement can be a powerful motivator. Treat yourself whenever you hit a milestone, whether maintaining a habit for a month or noticing tangible benefits.

Actionable Tip: Plan rewards in advance. It could be something simple like a favorite treat or a day off to indulge in a loved hobby.

Educate and Evolve: Continued success in maintaining habits often comes from staying updated. New research, techniques, or insights can add value to your practices.

Actionable Tip: Dedicate some time each month to read or watch content related to your habits. For example, if you're cultivating mindfulness, perhaps a new meditation technique or a seminar on its benefits might interest you.

Connect with Like-minded Individuals: There's strength in numbers. Being a part of a community that shares your goals or habits can be immensely motivating. Their journeys, challenges, and successes can offer both insights and encouragement. *Actionable Tip*: Join online forums, groups, or local clubs that resonate with your habits. Share, learn, and grow together.

Maintaining habits, especially those pivotal for empath well-being, is an ongoing journey. It's not just about the destination but the richness of the journey itself. As we transition to the next segment of this guide, remember that relationships play a crucial role in our well-being. The habits and routines you've cultivated now will act as a foundation, ensuring you navigate and enhance your empathic connections with others, solidifying bonds with mutual respect and understanding. The tools, strategies, and insights you've gathered will be instrumental in rekindling and fortifying these vital relationships.

8

NAVIGATING NARCISSISTIC STORMS WITH EMPATHY

Understanding the Role of Empathy in Difficult Relationships

While magnificent, our innate traits as empaths can sometimes pull us into the stormy waters of relationships with narcissists. They can be magnetically drawn since they sense our ability to understand, validate, and heal. For a narcissist, an empath can seem like an endless reservoir of emotional sustenance.

However, herein lies the delicate balance we must strike. While our empathy allows us to see and understand the pain and insecurity that often lies beneath the narcissist's behavior, it's essential not to get lost in their emotional turbulence. It's a dance of shadows and light—our empathy illuminates the vulnerabilities of the narcissist, but we must ensure that our light isn't overshadowed in the process.

One might wonder why empaths often find themselves in these dynamics. The answer is twofold. First, our desire to heal and to understand can make us hopeful. We might believe we can bring about change or awareness through compassion. Second, the narcissist, sensing this, can artfully mirror our deepest desires and feelings, creating a mirage of connection that can be intoxicating.

Yet, it's essential to remember that while we can acknowledge the narcissist's perspective, we must not lose sight of our self-worth. It's a delicate balancing act where we validate their feelings without invalidating our own. This might mean recognizing the narcissist's need for admiration without allowing it to eclipse our own need for respect and understanding.

As we tread these waters, staying anchored in our truth is crucial. Remember that our empathy, while a bridge to understanding others, should not become a pathway to losing ourselves. As the adage goes, "Not all that glitters is gold." Similarly, not every emotional connection, no matter how deep or intense, is nourishing or healthy.

Our progress ahead will guide us on how to navigate these relationships while preserving our emotional well-being. How do we set boundaries? How do we resolve conflicts? When and how should we consider disengaging? We'll explore these questions together, ensuring that our empathic gift remains our strength, not our vulnerability. As we venture into these dynamics, remember the essence of who you are—an empath with a heart full of compassion and a spirit that deserves respect and understanding.

The Empath's Guide to Setting Boundaries

Walking the tightrope of relationships with narcissists requires the strong support of well-established boundaries. This doesn't mean shutting ourselves off or looking the other way; it simply means ensuring that we can interact with integrity, holding space for our feelings alongside those of the narcissist.

Boundaries aren't barriers or walls meant to shut people out. Think of them as a protective circle, a space where you honor and respect your own needs, values, and emotions. This circle is essential for empaths, especially when in the company of those who might unconsciously try to take more than we give.

Narcissists can sometimes overstep. Their hunger for admiration can overshadow an empath's need for genuine connection. But here's the thing: it isn't about blaming or holding resentments. It's about recognizing patterns and adjusting our sails. This dance becomes more harmonious when we know our steps and maintain our rhythm.

Why Boundaries are Critical

For many empaths, setting boundaries can feel like an act of defiance or even selfishness. But it's quite the opposite. Boundaries are an act of self-respect and a testament to the value we place on mutual understanding in relationships. They ensure that our vast reservoirs of compassion and empathy are not drained but renewed and replenished.

By defining these boundaries, we also provide clarity for the narcissist. It's like charting out a map, indicating where the safe passages and treacherous terrains lie. In doing so, we protect ourselves and offer a structure within which a narcissist can engage without causing unintentional harm.

Establishing and Maintaining Boundaries

Self-awareness: Start by understanding what feels right and what doesn't. Listen to that inner voice. If a situation or interaction leaves you feeling drained or diminished, it's a sign to re-evaluate the boundaries in place.

Clear communication: Be clear about your needs. It's not about making demands, but more about expressing feelings. For instance, "I feel overwhelmed when we discuss this. Can we talk about it later?" provides space without shutting down communication.

Consistency: Once a boundary is set, it's crucial to maintain it. Consistency reinforces the importance of the boundary and ensures it's respected over time.

Engage with compassion: Remember, setting boundaries is not an act of aggression. Approach the subject with understanding, acknowledging the feelings of the narcissist while standing firm in your own needs.

Review and adjust: Our boundaries might need adjustments with everything in life. Regularly check in with yourself, assess your feelings in the relationship, and make necessary shifts.

In the intricate dance with narcissists, boundaries provide the choreography that ensures both partners can move gracefully, with minimized missteps. But what happens when conflicts arise, as they often do? How do we use our understanding of both our empathic nature and the narcissist's tendencies to find a resolution? As we forge ahead, we'll delve deeper into conflict resolution, ensuring we're not left adrift when storms come but can navigate them with skill and grace.

Conflict Resolution with the Narcissist

Conflicts are almost inevitable when two worlds as contrasting as those of empaths and narcissists intersect. However, while these confrontations might seem daunting, they're not insurmountable. The key lies in understanding, tact, and an unwavering commitment to one's emotional well-being. After my own experiences, other than years of observation, interaction, and, most importantly, learning, I have gathered a set of proven strategies to guide you smoothly through these rough tides. I sincerely hope that by sharing them, you can find solace and mastery in managing such conflicts.

Techniques to De-escalate Conflicts

Listening Actively: Remember that one of the primary needs of a narcissist is to feel heard and validated. As empaths, we possess a unique ability to tune into others' emotions, and this can be used as a tool. By actively listening, you're not just absorbing words but acknowledging the underlying emotions. This acknowledgment can often quell the rising storm, even before it truly begins.

Choose Your Battles: Not every disagreement warrants a battle. Sometimes, letting go is the most empowering choice. Ask yourself: "Is this conflict worth my energy? What do I hope to achieve?" By prioritizing your well-being, you can discern which issues to tackle and which to let slide.

Shift from Accusation to Expression: Instead of starting sentences with "You always..." or "You never...", lead with "I feel..." or "I observe...". This focuses on your feelings rather than placing blame, paving the way for a more constructive conversation.

Seek Common Ground: Remember, underneath the behaviors and tendencies of narcissism, there's a person with feelings and vulnerabilities. Finding a shared understanding or common point can act as an anchor in turbulent conversations.

Understanding the Narcissist's Emotional State

To effectively resolve conflicts with a narcissist, we must delve a bit deeper into their emotional landscape. We know narcissists often operate from a place of deep-seated insecurity and fear. Their behaviors, as perplexing as they might seem, are defense mechanisms. When they feel threatened or invalidated, they might lash out or become defensive. Recognizing this can provide a fresh perspective.

As empaths, it might be tempting to absorb this emotional turmoil. But here lies the challenge and the strength: to understand without internalizing, to empathize without drowning. This balance is your shield and mediator in conflicts.

Finding Middle Ground

A successful resolution doesn't always mean agreement. Sometimes, it's about finding a middle path where both parties feel respected. It's essential to approach these discussions with an open mind and heart, seeking solutions rather than victories. This might mean compromising on some fronts and standing firm on others, but always with the intention of mutual respect.

Remember, though, that continuously compromising at the expense of your well-being is not the goal. It's about finding a balance where both your needs and the narcissist's are considered.

Navigating conflicts with narcissists can indeed feel like traversing a maze. But equipped with understanding, patience, and the tools we've discussed, you'll find a path to calm even amid storms.

However, while resolution is the aim, it's also crucial to recognize when a relationship has veered off the course of mutual respect and understanding. In some cases, the healthiest choice might be to evaluate the sustainability of the relationship. As we progress, we'll explore the signs that indicate when it might be time to step back and prioritize one's emotional and mental well-being over sustaining the relationship.

Recognize When It's Time to Disengage

There's a moment amid the most vibrant storms where the clouds part just enough to let a sliver of sunlight through. That brief, fleeting instant can be a sign—a nudge from the universe that clarity is possible even amid chaos. I remember feeling this in the tumult of my relationship with a narcissist. Through the deafening roar of confusion and heartache, a whisper of truth reached me: sometimes, for our own well-being, we must let go.

Evaluating the Health of the Relationship

Navigating a relationship with a narcissist taught me vital life lessons. One of the most profound was the importance of self-assessment. As empaths, we're naturally attuned to the emotions of those around us. Still, it's crucial to tune into our feelings periodically.

Constant Emotional Exhaustion: There were days when every conversation felt like wading through quicksand. If your heart feels weary after every interaction, it's a sign worth noting.

Treading Lightly: I recall the caution with which I'd approach discussions, fearful of setting off another emotional mine. Love should never be a battlefield where you're always on the defensive.

Erosion of Self-Worth: There were moments I doubted my

worth, questioned my truth. A relationship should uplift, not undermine.

Feeling Isolated: When passions that once brought joy start fading, and friendships feel distant, it indicates that the relationship might be narrowing your world rather than enriching it.

Prioritizing Self-Love

In my journey, I realized the depths of my ability to love and understand others. But I also learned something equally transformative: the importance of self-love. It's a lesson I wish to share with every empath navigating the turbulent waters with a narcissist. Your heart, with its boundless capacity to heal, deserves care too.

There's no weakness in prioritizing oneself. When the scales of a relationship tilt so far that your well-being is in jeopardy, stepping back is not defeat. It's a brave act of self-preservation. If there's one thing I want you to take away from my experiences, it's that letting go can be the most profound act of love you can offer—both to yourself and the other person.

It's crucial to understand that choosing to disengage isn't about turning your back on love or care. It's about recognizing the patterns that don't serve our well-being and finding the strength to carve a path toward peace. The steps to walk away can be challenging, but they're integral in our quest for thriving. In the next segment, we'll explore strategies to help you should you find yourself at this juncture. Remember, every choice made in favor of your well-being is a step closer to a life of true harmony and fulfillment.

Strategies for Disengagement

Sometimes, the bravest journey we embark on is the one

away from what no longer serves us. I can't tell you the number of nights I spent wondering if I had the strength to chart a new course, away from a relationship that was slowly diminishing my spark. But with time, clarity, and a few trusted strategies, I forged a path towards healing. If you find yourself standing at the cross-roads, considering a departure from a narcissistic relationship, here's what I've learned and hope you find solace in:

Seek Clarity: Remember the introspection we discussed earlier? Begin there. Dedicate moments of stillness to ask yourself: *Is this relationship allowing me to thrive?* Sometimes, just asking the question brings us closer to the answers our hearts seek.

Safe Spaces and Trustworthy Ears: Lean into your support system. Whether it's a trusted friend, family member, or counselor, share your feelings. While navigating my departure, the insights and reassurances of loved ones acted like guiding stars.

Articulate without Blame: Clearly communicate your intent to disengage without pointing fingers. Focus on sharing your personal experiences and reasons for the decision, emphasizing the importance of mutual understanding.

Physical and Emotional Distance: Create some space. In my experience, this isn't always about moving cities or changing jobs. Still, maybe it's as simple as muting their chats or taking a few days off from interacting. A little distance provides perspective and reduces the intensity of emotions.

Affirmations and Self-compassion: During this phase, doubts might creep in. There were mornings I'd wake up questioning everything. In those moments, I leaned into affirmations.

Phrases like *"I am worthy of love and respect"* or *"It's okay to prioritize my well-being"* became my anchor.

Reconnect with Yourself: Rediscover the passions and hobbies that may have taken a backseat. It was returning to the tranquility of nature hikes and the joy of watercolor painting. These pursuits offered solace and a reminder of my essence.

Anticipate Grief: Walking away doesn't mean the love or care evaporates. Grieving is natural. It's a testament to the authenticity of your emotions. Be gentle with yourself during this phase. I allowed myself to cry, reminisce, and gradually heal.

As we move forward, it's essential to understand that disengaging doesn't signify a failure. Sometimes, the most profound love stories are the ones we write with ourselves. Recognize your strength in seeking what's best for your well-being.

I want to leave you with this thought: *growth often thrives in places of discomfort.* Just as the caterpillar must undergo a challenging metamorphosis to emerge as a butterfly, so too must we face our struggles head-on to realize our potential fully.

The subsequent stages will be about healing and recovery. As we dive into those realms, remember you're not walking alone. The path may have its shadows, but with resilience, guidance, and an empowered heart, you can—and will—find your way to a life of love, understanding, and boundless joy.

9

HEAL AND RECOVER FROM NARCISSISTIC RELATIONSHIPS

Grasp the Trauma of Narcissistic Behaviors

After a stormy evening, a certain peace comes from listening to the raindrops trace their paths on the window pane, each droplet carrying a story of the skies. Much like these remnants of a storm, the emotional aftershocks of navigating a relationship with a narcissist leave traces on our souls, each scar narrating tales of battles fought within and beyond.

I recall days when I'd find myself enveloped in self-doubt. Was it something I did? Could I have been more understanding? If you've been entwined in the complex dance with a narcissist, these questions might sound all too familiar. It's crucial at this juncture to illuminate the depth of the trauma that narcissistic behaviors can inflict, especially on the gentle and receptive hearts of empaths.

Each undermining comment, each passive-aggressive behavior, and each attempt to belittle or control isn't just an action; for the empath, it's an emotional wound that runs deep. Over time, these wounds can layer upon one another, creating a tapestry of trauma that may cloud our perception, judgment, and self-worth.

You see, the narcissist's behaviors — their need for constant admiration, sense of entitlement, and knack for exploiting others without remorse — aren't mere character quirks. They're powerful waves that can, if we're not anchored well, carry us into a sea of confusion, eroding our sense of self, bit by bit.

But, as we delve deeper into this abyss, let's not forget the resilience of the human spirit, especially that of an empath. I remember nights when I'd write down my feelings under a veil of tears, trying to make sense of the maze I was trapped within. These were my initial steps towards healing — acknowledging the trauma, understanding its roots, and preparing to rise above.

To anyone reading this, you might wonder if the pain, confusion, and trauma will ever cease. I've been there. And while it's not a journey you can rush, it's one that, with courage, support, and understanding, can lead you to places of profound healing and self-discovery.

We've explored the transformative power of vulnerabilities and the strength that stems from understanding ourselves better. The next step in this healing process is crafting shields — not walls that close us off. Still, shields that protect our essence ensuring we're not unduly influenced or hurt by those who might not have our best interests at heart.

Before we delve into building these protective layers, remember that every droplet and scar has a story. Understanding and honoring our past enables us to craft a brighter, more empowered future. The pain might be real, but so is the healing potential. Let's walk this path together, step by step, with hope and unwavering resolve.

Crafting a Shield Against Narcissistic Snares

On a personal retreat a few years ago, I had a beautiful experience of crafting a shield from nature's bounties. Weaving branches, flowers, and leaves, I created something that, while visually appealing, symbolized a deeper meaning for me: a shield against negative energies. Each element I incorporated held a purpose, much like the protective mechanisms we need against the emotional turbulence caused by narcissists.

Every empath also has within them the potential to build shields of resilience. These aren't barriers meant to block out the world but a protective embrace, ensuring our vulnerabilities aren't exploited.

Reflecting on my past encounters, I realize that one of the most effective shields against narcissistic snares is *knowledge.* When you can recognize the tell-tale signs of manipulation, gaslighting, or any other narcissistic behaviors, you can respond rather than react. You see, a narcissist thrives on the element of surprise, on catching you off-guard. When you can preempt their actions, you've already won half the battle.

Another vital component is *self-affirmation.* In my early days of navigating these stormy relationships, I often found myself with a little notebook. In it, I wrote down everything that made me, well, me. Every compliment I'd received, every achievement, no matter how minor, found its way onto these pages. In moments of doubt, when a narcissist's words threatened to overwhelm me, I'd turn to my little book of sunshine. It served as a reminder that I wasn't the problem; the behavior being thrust upon me was.

However, perhaps the most crucial shield is boundaries. I remember reading somewhere, *"Boundaries aren't about keeping others out but about cherishing what lies within"*. For an empath, this is of paramount importance. Our capacity to feel, to understand, to connect is a gift, but without boundaries, it can often become a curse. Setting clear, non-negotiable limits on what we will and will not tolerate ensures our emotional well-being is never compromised.

The creation of this shield is not a one-time event. Just as I had to mend and adjust my nature-crafted protection against the natural elements, we must continually refine our defenses against narcissistic behaviors. This ongoing process might seem daunting, but with each adjustment, we grow stronger, more resilient.

There were moments, nestled in the silvery embrace of the moonlight when I'd wonder if all this effort was worth it. Could I not just sever ties and live free from these challenges? But then, I'd remember the countless souls, much like you, dear reader, navigating these choppy waters, seeking guidance, solace, and strength. Our experiences, shared and individual, form a collective tapestry of resilience.

As we proceed, you'll see that healing from these scars sometimes necessitates seeking professional guidance. *There's no shame in asking for help.* I've walked that path, holding the hand of a counselor, and found it enriched with insights, understanding, and the promise of a brighter tomorrow. But before we delve into that, take a moment to appreciate the shield you've begun to craft.

It's a testament to your strength, your resolve, and the brilliant future that awaits.

The Healing Power of Professional Guidance

A dear friend once shared a beautiful analogy with me that resonated deeply, and I believe you'll find it illuminating. She said, "Imagine you're lost in a vast forest. The trees are dense, and every path looks eerily similar. You have a sense of where you need to go, but the thick canopy and the overlapping trails keep getting you turned around. Now, what if you had someone who's traveled these woods before? Someone who can guide you, not by telling you where to go, but by helping you see the landmarks and signs that have always been there."

This is what professional guidance feels like when navigating the tumultuous aftermath of a relationship with a narcissist. I remember when I first sought counseling; it was not out of a profound epiphany but rather sheer exhaustion. The emotional toll, the recurring patterns, the endless questioning— "Was it me? Could I have done something differently?"— all these whispers echoed in my mind, pulling me into a spiraling dance of self-doubt.

The first session was a revelation. Not because the therapist had all the answers but because they provided a safe space for my stories, pain, and confusion. They listened, truly listened, in a way that made me feel seen, understood and validated. Over time, this process of sharing, reflecting, and analyzing became a transformative journey. It was like piecing together a jigsaw puzzle with someone who knows that the bigger picture exists, even when you can't yet see it.

We often underestimate the intricacies of our psyche. While

self-awareness is crucial, there's a dimension of objectivity and structured guidance that professionals bring to the table. They're trained to recognize patterns, delve deeper into our subconscious behaviors, and offer tools and strategies tailor-made for our unique experiences.

As empaths, we have this innate desire to heal, mend, and bring things to harmony. Yet, sometimes, our internal compass can get clouded by external influences, especially after being in a narcissistic relationship. A professional becomes that beacon of light, guiding us back to our authentic selves.

It's crucial to remember that seeking therapy or counseling isn't an admission of defeat or weakness. Instead, it's a brave step towards self-awareness and healing. I recall the myriad of emotions I grappled with before taking this step: pride, fear, hope, and skepticism. But, with each session, I uncovered layers of myself that I had either forgotten or never known existed.

I want to emphasize the importance of rebuilding our sense of worth. While professional guidance provides the tools, the real magic happens when we apply these learnings, redefining our narrative and re-embracing our intrinsic value. I'll share some strategies and exercises that have helped me reclaim my self-worth after the scars of narcissistic wounds. But for now, cherish the steps you've taken, the strength you've shown, and the luminous path of healing you're embarking upon because you are worth every bit of love, respect, and happiness the universe holds.

Regaining Your Inner Worth After Narcissistic Wounds

In the cocoon of our experiences intertwined with narcissism, we often find ourselves questioning our worth. Sometimes, I felt bent to my breaking point like a delicate sapling under a relentless storm. The constant barrage of criticism, gaslighting, and subtle erosions of self-esteem left me doubting the very core of who I was. But here's the truth I want to share with you, from one empath's heart to another: *your worth is intrinsic and immutable, and no experience, no matter how painful, can take it away.*

After such intense emotional turbulence, I found solace and strength in several practices. These anchors guided me back to my core and reignited the spark of self-worth that had dimmed but never extinguished.

Reconnect with your passions: For me, it was the gentle strumming of my guitar, the feeling of paintbrushes against canvas, and the rhythm of words pouring onto paper. Delving into these passions reminded me of my essence beyond any external validation. What activities make you lose track of time? What hobbies once brought joy but have been pushed to the sidelines? Reconnect with them. They are not just pastimes but fragments of your soul, waiting to be pieced together.

Daily Affirmations: I started practicing standing in front of my mirror every morning, looking into my eyes, and repeating, "I am enough. I am loved. I am worthy." Initially, it felt silly, and there were days I didn't believe the words. But over time, they became my mantra, resonating deep within and creating ripples of positive self-belief.

Physical Reconnection: Whether it was the gentle flow of yoga, the intensity of a morning jog, or just long walks surrounded by nature, moving my body became therapeutic. It reminded me daily that I was alive, resilient, and in control of my vessel.

Journaling: While I've mentioned the transformative power of journaling before, I want to emphasize it again in this context. It's crucial because the act of writing serves as both a reflection and a compass. This was perhaps the most potent tool in my arsenal. Pouring my thoughts, fears, hopes, and dreams onto paper created clarity. It provided a tangible outlet for the intangible chaos within. Writing also allowed me to track my progress, see how far I'd come, and recognize patterns that needed attention.

Seeking Feedback: There's a tribe around each one of us – friends, family, mentors, or colleagues who've seen our brilliance, even when we've been blind to it. I reached out not for validation but for a reflection from trusted souls who reminded me of my strengths, achievements, and the difference I made in their lives.

Emerging from the shadows of narcissistic relationships can be likened to waking up from a deep slumber. There's initial disorientation, a yearning to return to the familiar, and fear of the unknown. Yet, with each passing day, the sun shines a little brighter, the path becomes more evident, and our stride regains its confidence.

The journey to re-establish our self-worth isn't linear. There'll be days of euphoric revelations and days when old wounds ache afresh. But with patience, love, and consistent effort, we can and will rediscover our radiant selves.

Remember, healing isn't just about moving on from the past but also about envisioning and shaping a future where you're the hero of your story, basking in the love and respect you so rightfully deserve. And as we turn the page, I want to celebrate this journey of recovery with you and envision a world free from toxic influences where our empathic souls can truly flourish.

Celebrate Recovery and Envision a Toxic-Free Future

A beautiful moment arrives after a storm, where the skies clear, and we glimpse the first rays of sunshine piercing through the lingering darkness. It's a scene I've witnessed in nature and metaphorically in my journey as an empath healing from narcissistic relationships. The rainbow after the rain isn't just a product of nature; it's the emblem of recovery, hope, and a brighter tomorrow. The voyage to this point has been grueling, but let us not forget to honor the sheer courage and determination that brought us here.

After numerous encounters with narcissistic influences, I found it was not just about healing old wounds. It was equally about embracing the dawn of a new era in my life, a chapter where I stood tall, embracing my scars and the lessons they brought. And, if you've reached this juncture in your journey and in this book, I want you to pause for a moment. Breathe deeply and celebrate yourself. Your tenacity, spirit, and the undying flame of hope you've clung to.

But how do we ensure that the healing doesn't stop here, and instead, we carry it forward into a bright, empowered future?

Visualizing a Future Free from Toxicity: Every morning, as I sip my tea, I spend a few minutes visualizing my day, my week, and my future. It's not about detailed plans but more about feelings and energy. I envision myself surrounded by love, positive energy, and supportive relationships. This simple act has a profound impact. When we can clearly visualize a life devoid of toxicity, we naturally steer ourselves in that direction.

Reinforce Boundaries: Celebrating recovery is not the end but rather a new beginning. As we step into a future free from narcissistic snares, our boundaries must be periodically revisited and reinforced. It's not about building walls but about ensuring that the sanctity of our emotional and mental space is preserved.

Nurture New Relationships: As we move ahead, we'll form new bonds and relationships. While the past might make us wary, remember to approach new connections with an open heart but with the wisdom of experience. Seek out those who resonate with our authentic self, who honor our journey, and with whom mutual respect and understanding flourish.

Keep the Growth Mindset Alive: One significant realization I had was that the growth mindset wasn't just for healing; it was for thriving. Every new day presents opportunities to learn, expand our horizons, and enrich our souls. Embrace them with open arms. Dive into new hobbies, read more, travel, and explore. Let every experience add layers to your beautiful soul.

Stay Connected to Your Empathic Nature: Our empathic nature, which makes us vulnerable to narcissists, is the same trait that makes us incredibly special. Cherish it. Use it as a beacon to guide others, to spread love and positivity, and to illuminate the world with your unique light.

As we transition to the next chapter, I want you to remember that forging ahead with empowerment isn't about forgetting the past. Instead, it's about using it as a stepping stone to reach greater heights. The journey ahead is promising and filled with endless possibilities. And as we step boldly into our empowered future, let's do it with grace, strength, and the undying belief in our inherent worth.

10

FORGE AHEAD WITH EMPOWERMENT

Reflect on Your Self-Discovery Journey

Embarking on the path of self-discovery is akin to navigating a labyrinth. There are twists and turns, moments of clarity, and instances of doubt. But every step, every challenge faced, has shaped you and led you to this very moment. As we enter this final chapter, it's essential to pause and look back, acknowledge the vast terrain you've traversed, and appreciate the resilience nurtured within you.

Life is not a linear progression but rather a series of peaks and valleys. Your journey as an empath, entangled with a narcissist or a dark empath, undoubtedly had its shadowed valleys. The weight of the emotional strain, the grappling with self-worth, and the moments where the path seemed too overgrown to continue were the testing grounds of your spirit. And yet, here you stand, not just a survivor but someone ready to thrive.

Reflection isn't just about remembering the struggles; it's

about recognizing the growth that has come from them. Think of the times you felt overwhelmed yet pushed forward. Recall the moments when you felt lost, only to find a new part of yourself that you hadn't known before. Each instance was a lesson, a stepping stone on your path to empowerment.

I, too, remember the days when the pain seemed impossible and the weight of someone else's emotional chaos threatened to drown my spirit. But in that pain and moments of utter vulnerability, I also found a clarity of purpose. It was in the fires of these trials that my determination was forged. And I believe, with all my heart, that your journey has similarly shaped you, molding you into an even more profound, empathic, and empowered individual.

But why is reflection so crucial, especially now? Because in understanding our past, we glean insights for our future. We can pinpoint the strategies that worked for us, recognize the triggers that once held power over us, and better equip ourselves for the future. In many ways, the rearview mirror holds the key to navigating the path forward with greater confidence and clarity.

Embrace this reflection, not just as a look back but as a celebration. Celebrate the courage you showed, the boundaries you set, and the love you gave—even when it wasn't reciprocated. And most importantly, celebrate the love you've started to show yourself.

As we move forward, hold onto these reflections. They remind you of your strength, signposts of how far you've come, and beacons for where you're headed. As we understand ourselves better, we become better equipped to cultivate relationships and environments that resonate with our true selves.

Commit to Continuous Learning

Life, with its intricate tapestry of experiences, is a perpetual classroom. It's a realm where every moment, every interaction, and every emotion holds a lesson. For empaths, this learning journey resonates deeply. With our heightened sensitivity to energies and emotions, we often find ourselves delving into layers of understanding that others might overlook. And this innate curiosity, this yearning for insights, becomes our beacon.

Several years ago, on a quiet evening, I found myself revisiting the pages of my old journal. Scribbled thoughts, raw emotions, and reflections stared back at me. As I traced my journey from being a vulnerable empath, overwhelmed by the world, to an empowered one, a pattern emerged. It was evident that every challenge, every heartbreak, and even every joy had taught me something pivotal. This realization was profound. It wasn't just about the experiences themselves but the introspection that followed. Committing to continuous learning was not just a choice but a lifeline.

Embracing this lifelong journey of learning isn't always straightforward. The world can be a cacophony of conflicting messages, leaving us unsure of which path to take. Yet, in these moments of uncertainty, our empathic nature becomes our guide. By tuning into our inner compass, we can discern the lessons that resonate with our core and filter out the noise.

But how does one nurture this commitment to continuous learning? The answer lies in embracing every experience as a teacher. Whether it's a conversation that broadens our perspectives, a book that challenges our beliefs, or even a meditation session that deepens our self-awareness, every moment holds growth potential.

A particular memory comes to mind—a workshop I had attended where the facilitator spoke about the fluidity of knowledge. "Imagine your understanding as water," she'd said, "It can flow, it can adapt, and most importantly, it can carve its path." It was a powerful analogy. As empaths, our ability to adapt and flow with experiences gives us an edge. But this fluidity needs to be channeled. It requires intent, focus, and a genuine desire to evolve.

One of the tools that have been invaluable in my quest for knowledge is mindful reflection. After each significant experience, I set aside quiet moments to introspect. What did I learn? How did it align with my journey? What can I do differently? This process, though simple, has transformed passive experiences into active lessons. It's made me a proactive participant in my own growth story.

Another equally essential aspect of this learning journey is sharing. As we delve deeper into our paths of self-discovery, sharing our insights and learnings with our community becomes vital. It's a two-fold process—while we offer our wisdom to others, their feedback and perspectives enrich us further. It's a symbiotic relationship where growth begets growth.

So, as we stand at the threshold of celebrating our achievements, it's essential to recognize that our victories aren't just a culmination of our efforts. They're a testament to our commitment to continuous learning, resolve to understand deeper, and passion to evolve relentlessly. Remember, as empaths, our journey is uniquely ours, but the lessons we glean have the power to illuminate not just our path but also the roads of those around us.

Celebrate Your Achievements

There was a moment, not too long ago, when I found myself standing on a quiet beach during sunset. The horizon bathed in hues of gold and purple, the waves gently caressing my feet, and a soothing breeze playing with my hair. As I stood there, enveloped by nature's embrace, I was overcome with gratitude. Each wave brought memories of past achievements, the challenges I had overcome, and the milestones I had reached. It was a moment of profound realization that our achievements, no matter how minuscule they may seem in the grand tapestry of life, deserve to be celebrated.

Life can often feel like a series of uphill battles, especially for empaths. We navigate the complexities of our heightened sensitivities, strive to create boundaries in relationships, and work diligently to transform vulnerabilities into strengths. Amidst this whirlwind of emotions and experiences, it becomes all too easy to overlook our achievements, brushing them aside as mere steps in our ongoing journey.

But here's the thing: Every step, every hurdle crossed, and every moment of resilience is a testament to our strength and perseverance. These aren't just achievements but badges of honor that tell tales of our courage and determination.

I recall a personal experience where I finally felt a semblance of balance after months of struggling with a particularly challenging phase in my life. I paused instead of rushing onto the next challenge, as was my usual demeanor. I celebrated that moment, not with grand gestures but with a quiet evening of reflection, accompanied by a cup of my favorite herbal tea and soft melodies playing in the background. That evening, I acknowledged my journey and rejoiced in my growth.

And this is where the magic lies. Celebrating our achievements isn't merely about external recognition but internal validation. It's about telling ourselves, "You did well. You grew. You conquered." It's an affirmation that bolsters our self-worth and propels us forward with renewed vigor.

So, how does one go about celebrating achievements? While grand celebrations have their place, the intimate, personal gestures often hold the most meaning. It could be penning down your feelings in a journal, sharing your journey with a close confidant, or even treating yourself to something you love. The key is recognizing and honoring your achievements in ways that resonate with you.

There's also immense power in sharing our victories with our tribe—the community that's been our pillar of strength. Celebrating together magnifies our joy and inspires others to acknowledge their achievements. These shared moments of joy create a ripple effect, touching lives and hearts in ways we can't even fathom.

As we stand on the cusp of stepping boldly into an empowered future, let's carry with us a heart full of gratitude and pride. Let's promise ourselves that we'll pause, reflect, and bask in the glory of our achievements, no matter how big or small. After all, these moments of joy and acknowledgment weave together to create the beautiful tapestry of our empowered empath journey.

Remember, every step, no matter how tiny, is a leap towards your empowered self. As we'll explore in the next section, these milestones, these celebrated moments, will form the backbone of our journey toward a future filled with empowerment and devoid of toxicity.

Step Boldly into an Empowered Future

As we reach the culmination of our introspective journey, it's essential to acknowledge that the path of healing, empowerment, and growth is not a destination but a lifelong endeavor. While the chapters of this book provide tools, insights, and guidance to navigate the often-tumultuous waters of relationships with narcissists and dark empaths, the true magic lies in embracing the life ahead with an open heart and unwavering spirit.

Every sunrise offers an opportunity to reinvent, rediscover, and reaffirm our commitment to personal growth. The power to shape our narrative, to transform wounds into wisdom, rests within us. It's about making an intentional choice every day: a choice to prioritize our well-being, a choice to surround ourselves with positivity, a choice to be our most authentic selves.

It's tempting to dream of a future where challenges don't exist. But the beauty of life lies in its unpredictability, in the myriad of emotions it evokes. Instead of seeking a life devoid of challenges, envision one where you're equipped with the knowledge and resilience to face anything that comes your way.

As we stand at the precipice of this new beginning, here's what I urge you to do:

Visualize Your Ideal Future: Take a moment to close your eyes. Imagine a world where you, as an empowered empath, thrive. How does it feel? What do you see? Who's there with you? By visualizing this ideal scenario, you're setting a subconscious intention, and your actions will naturally align to make this vision a reality.

Set Clear Intentions: While being flexible and open to life's myriad experiences is essential, setting clear intentions provides direction. These intentions could range from seeking therapy to joining empath communities or simply prioritizing self-care.

Stay Updated: The world of psychology and emotional well-being is continually evolving. New research, strategies, and insights emerge regularly. Stay updated. Attend seminars, read articles, or simply engage in conversations that expand your horizons.

Seek Joy in Small Moments: Empowerment isn't just about countering narcissists or setting boundaries; it's also about reveling in life's small joys. The fluttering of a butterfly, the aroma of the first rain, a child's innocent laughter. These moments, seemingly insignificant, have the power to fill our lives with unparalleled joy.

Remember, You're Not Alone: This journey of rediscovery and empowerment might seem daunting, but always remember, you're not alone. Thousands, if not millions, tread this path. They, too, seek solace, understanding, and a life of authenticity. Lean on each other. Draw strength from shared experiences. Grow together.

As we wrap up this guide, I want to share a small ritual I practice. Every evening, as the sun dips below the horizon, I light a small candle, its flame flickering and dancing. To me, it symbolizes hope, resilience, and the promise of a brighter tomorrow. As you step into your empowered future, may you always carry this flame within, guiding, warming, and reminding you of your incredible journey.

Your life, dear empath, is a magnificent tapestry of emotions, experiences, and memories. Every thread, color, and pattern has a unique story. While some parts of this tapestry might be wrought with pain, confusion, or chaos, these imperfections make it uniquely yours and beautiful. Remember, the path of an empath is like the river—it's fluid, ever-changing, and brimming with depth. As you forge ahead, may your journey be filled with enriching experiences, boundless love, and infinite growth. Embrace every facet of it, for the most profound lessons lie in the heart of challenges. As you step boldly into your future, know that you carry with you the collective wisdom of every experience, every tear, every moment of joy. From one empath to another, here's to our bright future.

You are ready. You are empowered.

And the world awaits your magic.

ACKNOWLEDGMENTS

As I sit back and reflect on the journey that culminated in this book, I am astonished with gratitude. Writing this wasn't just about sharing knowledge; it was a profoundly personal journey intertwined with countless stories, emotions, and insights.

Firstly, I must express my heartfelt gratitude to my family. Their unwavering support, faith, and love have been the pillars on which I've built my dreams. Their belief in me, even during times of doubt, was the beacon that illuminated my path.

Thank you to all the brave souls who shared their stories with me, allowing me to delve deep into their personal experiences, vulnerabilities, and triumphs. Your courage, resilience, and authenticity breathed life into this book, resonating with countless others seeking solace and empowerment.

A big shoutout to all the empath communities and support groups, both online and offline, that have been a constant source of inspiration. These communities' collective strength, wisdom, and warmth are truly awe-inspiring.

Lastly, to you, dear reader. Thank you for embarking on this journey with me, trusting my words, and seeking a brighter, empowered future. I wrote this book with the vision of it being a beacon of hope and a guide to strength. If it resonated with you, I've achieved my purpose.

THANK YOU